WORLD POPULATION
AND FOOD SUPPLY

WORLD POPULATION AND FOOD SUPPLY

J. H. LOWRY, M.A., B.Sc. (Econ.)
Senior Geography Master, Cranleigh School

Edward Arnold (Publishers) Ltd.

First published 1970
Reprinted 1971

ISBN: 0 7131 1597 1

Printed in Great Britain by
William Clowes & Sons, Limited, London, Beccles and Colchester

Preface

The aim of this book is to give an up-to-date account of all the problems which must be considered in discussing world food supply. Although the author does not subscribe to the gloomy predictions of many neo-Malthusians, the fundamental issues of an 'explosive' increase in the world's population are first analysed and an attempt is made to estimate foreseeable food requirements. Accepting that massive increases in food supply are urgently necessary the enquiry then examines the possibilities of extending and intensifying world agriculture and of producing unconventional and synthetic foodstuffs.

Revolutionary changes in agricultural techniques are currently affecting huge areas, notably in the older farmlands of temperate latitudes, but also increasingly in tropical and underdeveloped regions. This book brings together information on a wide range of new techniques, ideas and experiments—mainly but not exclusively biological and agricultural—not at present readily available to the student of human geography.

In producing a book at a time of transition to the metric system one is faced with the difficulty that much existing published information makes use of British units of measurement. The method adopted in this book is to use metric units throughout, except in some quoted passages where non-metric units are employed in the sources from which the quotations are taken. In a few cases both metric and British units are used for clarity.

When preparing a work of this kind one needs to lean heavily on the research records of a large number of specialists, and I am very grateful to all those who have given permission to quote from their published material.

The text is suitable for advanced study in secondary schools and as an introductory book for university students. Also, the wealth of thought-provoking information should prove invaluable to General and Liberal Studies groups.

J. H. L.

Contents

Section 1. World population

1. Growth and trends

Chart A pin-points the most urgent problem of the modern world. During the past century or so mankind has multiplied at an extraordinary and accelerating rate. Notice that whereas it took 200 years for the total world population to double itself after 1650, it took only 100 years after 1850. Notice, too, the remarkably short interval it will take to double itself from its present size, according to the predictions in the chart. This phenomenal increase in numbers lies at the root of many of the world's most pressing economic problems, for it involves an ever-increasing pressure of population on the limited material resources of the Earth, in many regions leading directly to hunger, poverty and disease. Furthermore population pressures are often the underlying cause of social and political unrest within a state and an excuse for expansionist foreign policies. In recent history, for example, an alleged lack of *lebensraum* (living-space) was an avowed basis of Nazi aggression, whilst both Italy and Japan fought to establish overseas colonies partly in order to settle land-hungry peasant-farmers from their congested homelands. Because the 'population explosion' is such a vital factor in any discussion of Man's relationship to his physical environment it is convenient to begin a study of Human Geography from this standpoint.

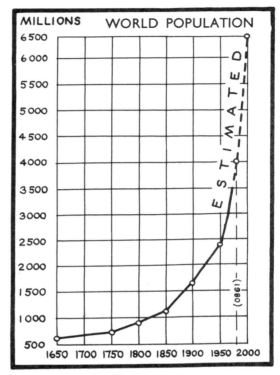

Chart A

Chart B overleaf shows the growth of population in England, Wales and Scotland since 1700. The pattern of this curve is highly significant, for with certain reservations it typifies changes which

Table I

ENGLAND AND WALES: BIRTH, DEATH AND INFANT MORTALITY RATES[1] AND LIFE EXPECTANCY									
		1851		1901		1931		1961	1968[2]
Birth rate per 1000 population		34·3		28·5		15·8		17·6	16·9
Death rate per 1000 population		22·0		16·9		12·3		11·9	11·9
Infant mortality per 1000 live birth occurrences		153		151		66		21	18
Life Expectancy[3] 1838–54		1901–10		1930–32		1950–52		1960–62	
	Male	Female	M	F	M	F	M	F	M	F
At birth	39·9	41·9	48·5	52·4	58·7	62·9	66·4	71·5	68·1	74·0
At age 21	38·8	39·6	42·2	44·9	46·0	49·0	48·7	53·2	49·6	55·0

[1] The Registrar General's Annual Reports (or Statistical Reviews from 1911) for England and Wales.
[2] The Registrar General's Weekly Return for Week Ended 31.1.1969 (provisional data).
[3] English Life Tables Nos. 3, 7, 10, The Registrar General's Decennial Supplement 1931, Pt. III, Table 9; English Life Tables No. 11, The Registrar General's Decennial Supplement 1951 English Life Tables No. 12, The Registrar General's Decennial Supplement 1961.

have affected most other Western nations, e.g. France, Germany, Belgium, the U.S.A. and the 'white' countries of the British Commonwealth. Population curves of these countries all show sudden and very rapid increases lasting several decades in the 19th century, followed by a gradual decrease in net reproduction rates. At a later stage the population may become static in numbers or even show a net decrease, as happened in France in 1911–13 and in 1938. In recent years the population curves of most Western countries show a return to a more rapid growth.

There is no single or simple explanation of 'population explosions', but except where migration into a country is exceptionally heavy[1] the principal factor is a marked decrease in the death rate. For Great Britain this is clearly indicated in Table 1, p. 1, and in Chart F, p. 5. The reader should work out the percentage changes which have occurred in (a) death-rates, (b) infant mortality rates and (c) life expectancy, between the earliest and latest given dates. 19th-

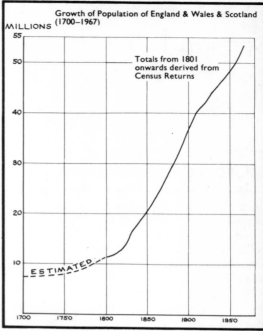

Chart B

century tombstones with inscriptions similar to that on the right can be found throughout the country: they are grim reminders that until comparatively recent times people in Britain lived

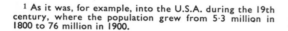

SOME FACTORS CONTRIBUTING TO A DECLINE IN THE DEATH RATE IN GREAT BRITAIN

Social Legislation, e.g.

1848   Boards of Health established (following London cholera epidemic of 1847–8) to provide mains drainage, a pure water supply and street cleaning facilities.

1850   Cesspools abolished in the City of London.

1868   Artisans' and Labourers' Dwellings Act—local authorities empowered to condemn property as unfit for habitation.

1875   Public Health Act established local sanitary districts. Sanitary authorities required to appoint medical officers of health, surveyors and sanitary inspectors.

1907   Act required births to be notified within 48 hours. Attempts to establish efficient midwives training scheme.

1911   National Insurance against sickness.

1921   Local councils made responsible for treating persons with tuberculosis.

1946   National Health Service Act made free medical services available to everybody in England and Wales.

Advances in Medical Science, e.g. introduction of vaccination against smallpox (1796). Inoculation hospital set up in London. Improvements in surgery, midwifery and military hygiene. Foundation of hospitals: between 1700 and 1825 154 new hospitals and dispensaries were established, including most of the famous London teaching hospitals.

Gradual Increase in Food Supply and Rise in Nutritional Standards, partly due to (i) 18th-century improvements in agriculture, e.g. stockbreeding; introduction of four-course 'Norfolk' rotation of crops; land drainage schemes; manuring; use of new agricultural implements, e.g. seed drills and cultivators, and (ii) cheap imports of grain from the New World after 1870.

Social Changes, e.g. availability of cheap washable cotton clothing after 1750 made personal cleanliness easier and so reduced infection.

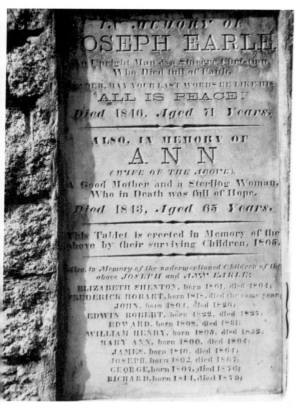

(Above) *Tombstone, Falmouth Parish Churchyard.*

(Below left) *Slums in Karachi, West Pakistan. Densely packed shanty-towns such as this are commonplace in the rapidly growing cities of under-developed regions. With no sewage disposal facilities the incidence of disease is inevitably high.*

(Below right) *Men bathing at a hydrant in a Calcutta street. Note the dirty open drain, cattle and debris. Dense overcrowding, inadequate sewers and the use of contaminated water for drinking and cooking help make Calcutta an endemic plague spot for cholera and smallpox.*

under appallingly unhealthy conditions.* With no knowledge of elementary hygiene, no piped water, no effective sewage disposal and virtually no medical science, it was little wonder that people were riddled with disease and early death was commonplace. Conditions were worst in the growing industrial towns, where polluted water supplies coupled with gross overcrowding in factories and dingy 'back-to-back' terrace houses gave full scope for epidemics such as smallpox, cholera, diphtheria and scarlet fever. Squalid slum conditions and malnutrition are now mainly associated with parts of 'under-developed' countries like India, Brazil and Egypt, but it is salutary to remember how widespread they were in Britain and other 'advanced' nations only a few decades ago.

Economic and socio-medical improvements similar to those listed opposite for Great Britain have long been operative throughout the Western world and are now becoming increasingly available to most of mankind. The population curves for India, Venezuela and China (*see overleaf*) are clearly akin to that of 18th–19th century Britain. In fact death rates are falling to such an extent that

... in a world which since the beginning of history has sustained terrible visitations of plague, cholera, smallpox and diphtheria, there has not been a major pandemic since 1919, when influenza is believed to have caused 25 million deaths around the world. In other words, world and national population growth has shifted from a wave-like pattern of gains and losses to a steady rapid upward trend. In consequence of these changes, a fertility rate which only a few generations ago was essential to mere survival, now results in a rapid

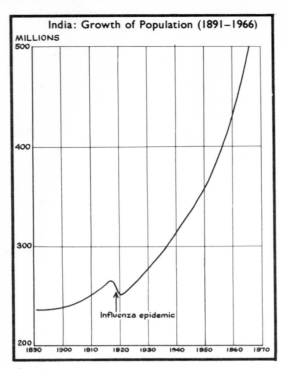

India: Growth of Population (1891–1966)

MILLIONS

Influenza epidemic

Chart C

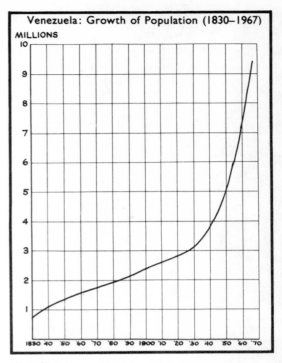

Venezuela: Growth of Population (1830–1967)

MILLIONS

Chart D

multiplication of numbers, by reason of ever better control of mortality. Through all of Man's previous history only a fraction of all the babies born had grown to maturity; now, in the industrial countries of the West, only 5 per cent die before adulthood. While six to eight children per woman were once necessary to maintain human numbers, today only a fraction over two children per woman are necessary to maintain a stable population in the industrial countries.[1]

The flattening out of the population curve for Great Britain early in the 20th century (*see Chart B, page* 2) was caused by a decrease in birth rates which gradually offset the continuing decrease in death rates. A similar decline in birth rates affected most other Western industrial countries following their population explosions. Reasons for this decline are complex, but it seems clear that a major factor was the invention of efficient methods of birth control and their gradual spread throughout an increasingly sophisticated society. Deliberate limitation of the size of families is mainly practised to avoid the burden imposed on women by a large family and to enable people more fully to enjoy the material benefits of modern civilization: by restricting the number of

births a higher living standard can be ensured. The emancipation of women in Western society also encourages more couples to choose smaller families, so that the wife can follow an occupation after a period of looking after young children. Other less tangible social and psychological influences are also at work in an educated society, for the size of families is subject to fashion and political persuasion. The security of a society may also affect birth rates, e.g. in the 'frontier' days of American history it was considered essential to have six or more children, whereas

Chart E

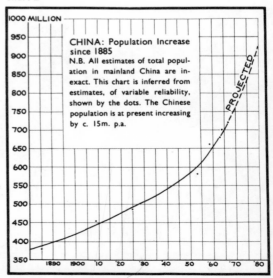

CHINA: Population Increase since 1885
N.B. All estimates of total population in mainland China are inexact. This chart is inferred from estimates, of variable reliability, shown by the dots. The Chinese population is at present increasing by c. 15m. p.a.

PROJECTED

1000 MILLION

[1] United Nations Office of Public Information, *Population and Food Supply*, p. 2.

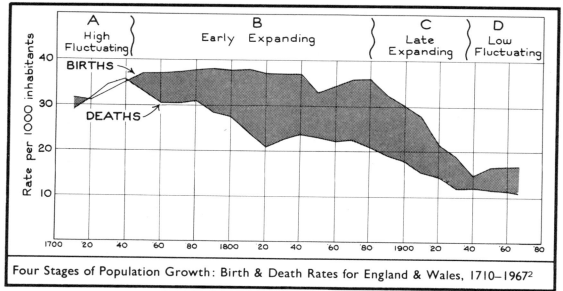

Four Stages of Population Growth: Birth & Death Rates for England & Wales, 1710–1967[2]

Chart F

[2] After Mountjoy, A. B. *Industrialisation and Under-developed Countries*, 1963.

It is frequently suggested that demographic growth takes place in a number of distinct stages, the stages being referred to collectively as the population cycle. This concept derives from European experience such as that for England and Wales represented in Chart F. The four stages indicated there are typical of Western countries which have undergone technological and social revolutions. It is also possible to place non-Western countries into one or other of the stages of a European-type cycle, but it should be noted that it is by no means certain that countries such as Ceylon (Chart G) which show population changes analogous to those of stages A and B will eventually evolve into stages C and D. Many countries at present have high birth rates coupled with sharply declining death rates, with correspondingly startling rates of natural increases. Examples include Tunisia (41·1 per thousand), El Salvador (44·2), Mexico (42·7), Venezuela (41·3) and Ceylon (31·5). A population with an annual rate of increase of 30 per thousand will double itself in 23 years.

today families of half that size are socially acceptable.

Compensatory decreases in birth rates, with resulting moderation in population growth, now extend over most of Europe, Anglo-America, temperate South America, Japan, Australasia and the Soviet Union. They are *not* yet evident, however, in rapidly multiplying 'underdeveloped' countries such as India, Pakistan, Brazil, Egypt and Congo. This is one of the most sobering aspects of the world population problem, for it is precisely these relatively very poor and mainly peasant communities that stand to lose most by a continuing upward surge in total numbers.

The rates of natural increase at present exceed three per cent in many of the countries in the less developed regions—enough to double the population in twenty-five years or less. In a few countries the increase even approaches a

Chart G

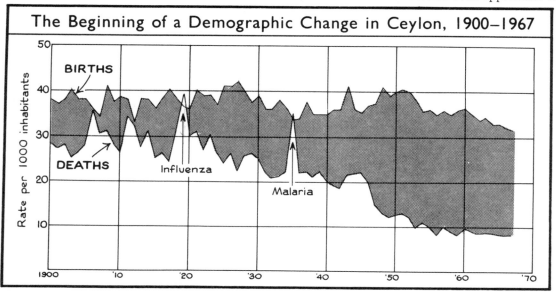

The Beginning of a Demographic Change in Ceylon, 1900–1967

6

rate of four per cent. As low death rates are extended over wider and wider areas, it appears likely that increases of more than three per cent a year will soon be the rule in the under-developed regions which contain two-thirds of the earth's inhabitants. The continuation of high fertility in the face of the reduction of mortality, particularly in the economically less advanced regions, is the crux of the population problem in the world today, and is an integral and essential factor in any realistic approach to the food outlook.[1]

This problem is well illustrated, for example, in the recent pattern of birth and death rates in Ceylon: details are given in Chart G (*page 5*).

As well as adding to the economic burden of less-well-off countries, variations in population increase also have grave social and political implications for multiracial states in which there is a 'colour bar' and racial hostility. For example, rates of increase are strikingly different for white and non-white populations in South Africa (*see Chart I*). Most observers agree that the fear of being 'overwhelmed' by the rapidly increasing Bantu is the main driving force behind the 'apartheid' policy of the South African government. Notice in the chart the extent to which the

proportion of whites to non-whites in South African has altered during this century. A difficult racial situation also exists in the U.S.A., where Negroes constitute approximately 11 per cent of the total population. In marked contrast to South Africa, however, the rate of growth of the American Negro population has recently slackened (*see Chart J*). Reasons for this deceleration are obscure, but may reflect a tendency for Negroes in the U.S.A. to restrict the size of their families because of a keenly felt sense of 'second-rate citizenship'.

On a world scale variations in rates of population increase have long-term strategic significance. The total number of people in the Communist 'bloc' already greatly outnumbers those in the non-Communist 'Western Alliance', and this unbalance will rapidly become more marked if the Chinese continue to multiply at their present rate (*see Chart E, p. 4*). The eagerness of the Americans to keep a lead in nuclear weapon technology in part reflects this inferiority in man-power. Even so the Chinese claim that they, alone amongst world powers, could survive a full nuclear onslaught by virtue of their enormous numbers and the vastness of their territory.

Changes in birth and death rates have important repercussions on the age distribution of a population. Age distribution is the proportion of a population in the various age groups, e.g. 0–4,

[1] United Nations Office of Public Information, op. cit.

Chart H

Work out the percentage increases in population between 1930 and 1967 for each of the regions shown in this diagram. Which of these regions would you classify as (a) economically advanced and (b) economically underdeveloped?

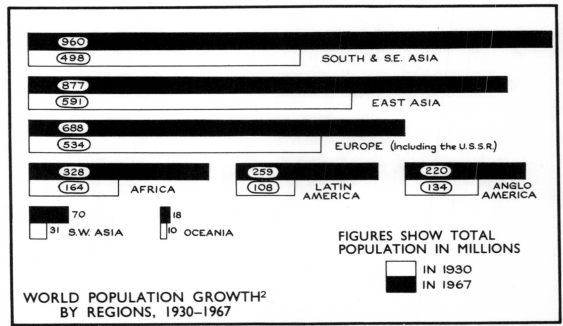

WORLD POPULATION GROWTH[2]
BY REGIONS, 1930–1967

[2] U.N. Demographic Year Book, 1967.

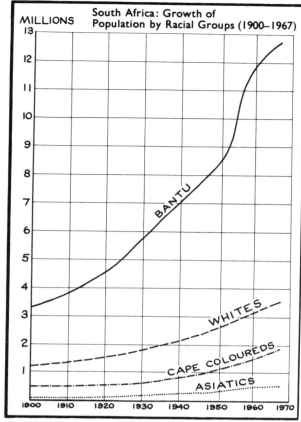

Chart I

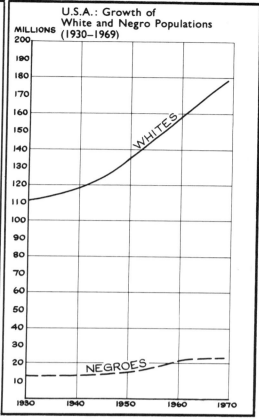

Chart J

5–9, 10–14, 15–19 and so on. Changes in these proportions can be conveniently illustrated by means of population 'pyramids', examples of which are given below. A population in which birth and death rates are both high gives a broad-based pyramid rapidly tapering towards the top. This is because although many children are born, a large proportion of them die in infancy, relatively few reach maturity and there are few old people. This situation is typified in the pyramid shown for England and Wales in 1841.

With decreasing death rates (notably amongst the very young) a pyramid broadens in its lower age-groups, for more and more infants survive to maturity: this condition is seen in the pyramid for England and Wales in 1891. A population such as this contains a relatively large number of young people and so has the economic advantage of possessing a vigorous, expanding labour force. In time, however, as birth rates begin to decline, the pyramid narrows at its base and this contraction gradually shifts upwards into the youthful

Chart K

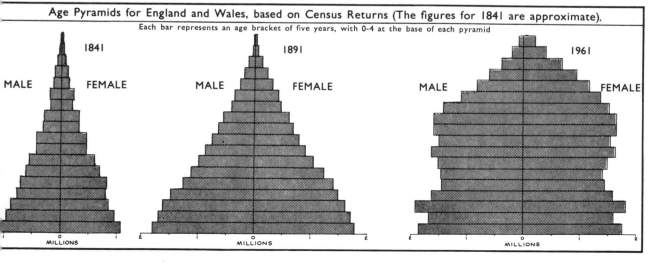

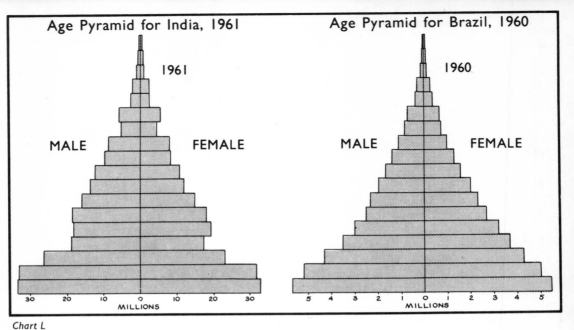

Age Pyramid for India, 1961   Age Pyramid for Brazil, 1960

Chart L

Chart M

Death rates in 102 Countries or Provinces: 1963–64 and 1965–66. (Rates[1] are the average number of deaths per 1000 population.)

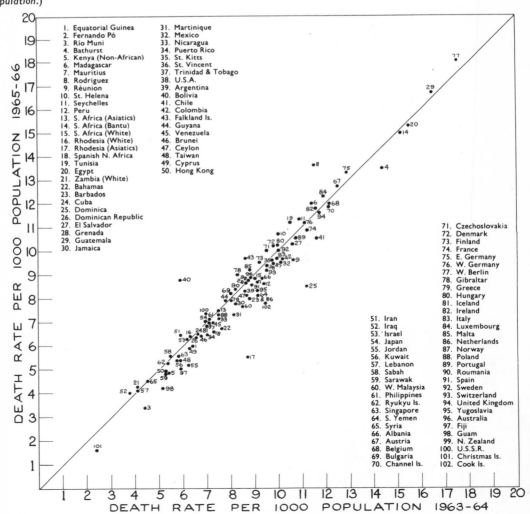

1. Equatorial Guinea
2. Fernando Pó
3. Río Muni
4. Bathurst
5. Kenya (Non-African)
6. Madagascar
7. Mauritius
8. Rodriguez
9. Réunion
10. St. Helena
11. Seychelles
12. Peru
13. S. Africa (Asiatics)
14. S. Africa (Bantu)
15. S. Africa (White)
16. Rhodesia (White)
17. Rhodesia (Asiatics)
18. Spanish N. Africa
19. Tunisia
20. Egypt
21. Zambia (White)
22. Bahamas
23. Barbados
24. Cuba
25. Dominica
26. Dominican Republic
27. El Salvador
28. Grenada
29. Guatemala
30. Jamaica

31. Martinique
32. Mexico
33. Nicaragua
34. Puerto Rico
35. St. Kitts
36. St. Vincent
37. Trinidad & Tobago
38. U.S.A.
39. Argentina
40. Bolivia
41. Chile
42. Colombia
43. Falkland Is.
44. Guyana
45. Venezuela
46. Brunei
47. Ceylon
48. Taiwan
49. Cyprus
50. Hong Kong

51. Iran
52. Iraq
53. Israel
54. Japan
55. Jordan
56. Kuwait
57. Lebanon
58. Sabah
59. Sarawak
60. W. Malaysia
61. Philippines
62. Ryukyu Is.
63. Singapore
64. S. Yemen
65. Syria
66. Albania
67. Austria
68. Belgium
69. Bulgaria
70. Channel Is.

71. Czechoslovakia
72. Denmark
73. Finland
74. France
75. E. Germany
76. W. Germany
77. W. Berlin
78. Gibraltar
79. Greece
80. Hungary
81. Iceland
82. Ireland
83. Italy
84. Luxembourg
85. Malta
86. Netherlands
87. Norway
88. Poland
89. Portugal
90. Roumania
91. Spain
92. Sweden
93. Switzerland
94. United Kingdom
95. Yugoslavia
96. Australia
97. Fiji
98. Guam
99. N. Zealand
100. U.S.S.R.
101. Christmas Is.
102. Cook Is.

age brackets. Meanwhile the decreased death rate allows increasing numbers of people to reach old age: thus in time the population is faced with the problem of a declining labour force and an increasing number of non-productive old-age pensioners. This situation is represented in the pyramid for England and Wales for 1961.

The present-day population pyramids for India and Brazil (*see Chart L, left*) are very similar to that for England and Wales in 1841. It remains to be seen whether there will be a significant fall in birth rates leading to a contraction at the base of such pyramids in the foreseeable future. The Indian government has mounted a large-scale birth control campaign during the past twenty years. Lecturers and demonstrators have travelled throughout the country exhorting peasant farmers to limit the size of their families. As yet, however, little progress seems to have been made, for the Indian population continues to multiply at a steady rate of 13 million annually. Peasant communities everywhere are well known for their conservative outlook and suspicion of new ideas and techniques. For centuries it has been an economic necessity for peasants to have many children, to ensure a labour force and to look after old folk when they can no longer support themselves. In India there is an added complication in that a Hindu, according to his religious faith, must ensure that when he dies a male heir will be at hand to perform funeral rites: Hindus therefore consider it important to have many sons. In most peasant communities, too, a large family is a mark of honour, a considerable status symbol and living testimony to one's virility and importance. Birth control enthusiasts find it difficult to make much headway against social and religious pressures of this kind. Even when the peasants accept the need for control they often find it difficult to follow instructions due to their ignorance and illiteracy.

Chart M shows the trends in death rates in all countries for which records were available in the mid 1960's.[1] The dots on the diagonal show no change. Those below the diagonal show a decline in death rate.

In many communities, both advanced and underdeveloped, people refrain from practising birth control because of religious objections. The greatest single factor in this respect is the teaching of the Roman Catholic Church, which expressly

[1] Source: U.N. Demographic Yearbook, 1967.

forbids its adherents from using any 'unnatural' methods of contraception. Birth rates are therefore significantly higher in Western Catholic countries such as Ireland and Spain than in Protestant states like Great Britain and Sweden. Roman Catholics predominate, too, in many underdeveloped countries, notably in Latin America and parts of Africa. Many populations in these territories are multiplying rapidly (*see, e.g., Chart D, p. 4*), resulting in overcrowding, hunger and poverty. In such a context the strict religious sanctions against birth control may seem harsh and unrealistic. This situation has recently caused serious misgiving and a crisis in allegiance within the Catholic Church, but it seems unlikely that official Church policy will be modified in the foreseeable future.

2. The distribution of world population

The map overleaf shows that Man is distributed very unevenly over the surface of the Earth. The reasons are mainly geographical, for through the centuries people have settled and multiplied mainly in those regions with natural resources best suited to sustain human life. As most of the world's people are farmers, obtaining their livelihood directly from the soil, this means living in a relatively fertile, well-watered region with a climate suitable for growing crops or rearing livestock.

One of the most significant events to influence the growth and distribution of mankind was the discovery of how to grow crops, i.e. the Neolithic Revolution. Archaeological evidence shows that this evolved simultaneously about 6000 years ago in the great river basins of Mesopotamia, Egypt and Monsoon Asia. The new techniques afforded cultivators a relative abundance of food, compared with the meagre and uncertain yield of people dependent on hunting and collecting. As the standards of diet and nutrition among cultivators improved they gradually multiplied and spread over all the best accessible farmland.

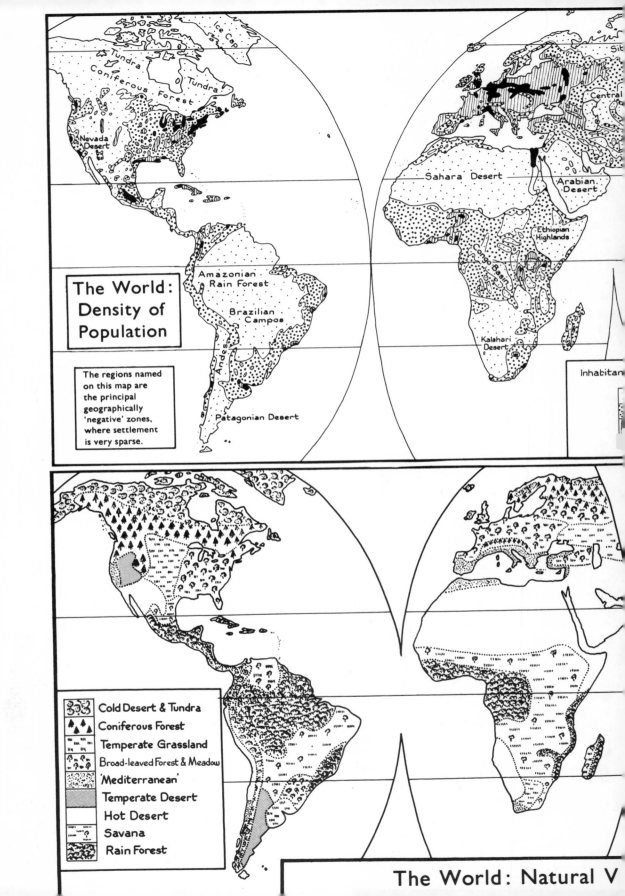

The World: Density of Population

Ice Cap

Tundra

Coniferous Forest

Tundra

Nevada Desert

Amazonian Rain Forest

Brazilian Campos

Andes

Patagonian Desert

The regions named on this map are the principal geographically 'negative' zones, where settlement is very sparse.

Sahara Desert

Arabian Desert

Ethiopian Highlands

Congo Basin

Kalahari Desert

Central

Sit

Inhabitan

Legend (Natural Vegetation):

- Cold Desert & Tundra
- Coniferous Forest
- Temperate Grassland
- Broad-leaved Forest & Meadow
- 'Mediterranean'
- Temperate Desert
- Hot Desert
- Savana
- Rain Forest

The World: Natural V

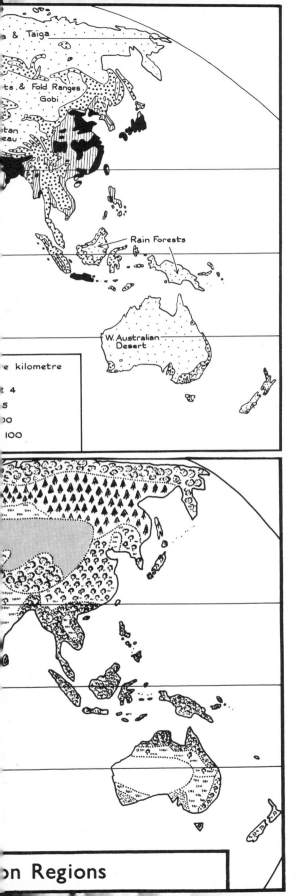

& Taiga

ts. & Fold Ranges
Gobi

tan
eau

Rain Forests

W. Australian
Desert

e kilometre

R 4

5

00

100

on Regions

Today the river basins of Monsoon Asia constitute one of the most densely populated regions in the world. Its 1800 million inhabitants —more than one-half of all mankind—are mostly peasant farmers, vitally dependent for their livelihood on irrigated rice cultivation. As settlement extended to the limits of the fertile river flood plains (*see photo*) the pressure of people on land resources steadily mounted. Farming methods therefore became very intensive in order to wring maximum yields from every scrap of soil. Great care is taken to maintain soil fertility by digging in all organic waste, including human manure. Elaborate hand methods of sowing, planting, weeding, irrigation and harvesting are still in general use, and so most people are directly involved in the production of foodstuffs. This age-old system of subsistence irrigation farming is extraordinarily well adapted to the seasonal fluctuations of the Monsoon climate, but now the impact of falling death rates (*see, for example, Chart G on page* 5) is throwing it into disarray. Faced with ever increasing populations, feverish efforts are being made, e.g. under the Indian Government's 'Five Year Plans', to boost agricultural production, but every advance in farming is offset by the arrival of new mouths to feed. Densely populated agrarian economies, very similar to those of Monsoon Asia and beset with similar problems of congestion and malnutrition, exist in the Nile Delta, Java and the Philippines. In the mountainous islands of Java and the Philippines an elaborate series of padi-fields is carved out of terraced hill slopes (*frontispiece photo*). The fertility of some Javanese rice-growing plots is revitalized annually by the downwash of mineral-rich volcanic ash from the island's interior.

The upper map shows that Europe is another

Flood plain padi-fields in Taiwan.

12 region with a high density of population. To a
certain extent this reflects, as in S.E. Asia, the
fertility of the land and the general favourability
of the continent for farming. In particular there
is an old-established and densely peopled belt of
farmland on the rich loess soils which reach
across the entire continent from the Ukraine to
the Paris Basin. (*See map below.*) In Europe,
however, there are also many very densely
populated industrial regions. The maps (*right*)
show that the location of these regions is closely
related to the distribution of minerals, especially
coal and iron ore. The reasons for this date back
about 250 years—to the first successful smelting
of iron ore using coke instead of charcoal in the
blast furnace, and to the invention of the steam
engine. Both these key discoveries were made in
Britain, and it was there that they first began to
revolutionize industry. Coalfields rapidly became
major industrial centres. Factories of all kinds
were built on them so as to be near the source of
power to drive their machines: iron and steel mills
needed coking coal; and metal-working engineering industries were located close to the supplies
of iron and steel. Thus developed the grimy,
noisy, bustling industrial towns of the 'Steel
Age'. Into them flocked tens of thousands of
people from the surrounding countryside.

The new ideas spread in time to the Continent,
and the maps opposite show the effects of coalfield industrial development on the distribution of
population. Map A shows the main bituminous
coal and lignite deposits in Europe. Tens of
millions of people live in industrial towns
located on or near these coalfields. In certain
places individual towns have grown to such an
extent that they have fused with each other to
form a continuous zone of built-up land called a
conurbation. Maps C and D overleaf show the
extent of the conurbations of the West German
Ruhr and the English 'Black Country'. Map B
shows the other main European conurbations.

The European coalfields did not all acquire
their dense urban populations at the same time.
First was the Franco-Belgian coalfield, which
developed rapidly from the late 18th century
onwards, partly under the direct supervision of
skilled British craftsmen and engineers who
settled there. German coalfields, by contrast, did
not become major industrial centres until late in
the 19th century. The main reason was that until
then the German lands were divided into a large
number of small, independent and economically
weak kingdoms. Unification under Prussia led to
the creation in 1870 of a powerful nation-state,
and from then until the First World War
Germany went all out to build up her heavy
industry. From 1871 until 1918 Germany

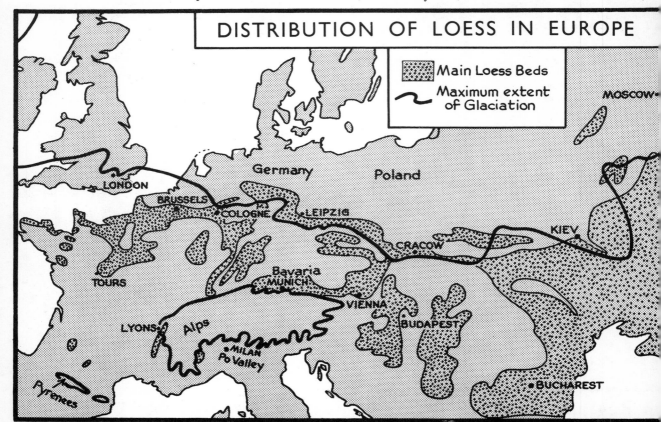

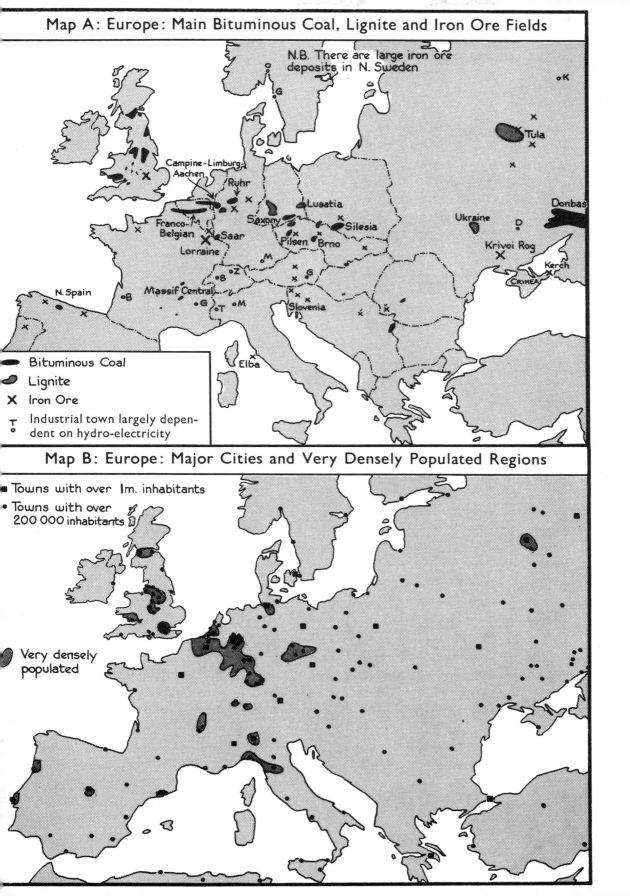

Map A: Europe: Main Bituminous Coal, Lignite and Iron Ore Fields

N.B. There are large iron ore deposits in N. Sweden

- oK
- x Tula x
- x
- Donbas
- Campine-Limburg-Aachen
- Ruhr x
- x Lusatia
- Saxony
- Silesia
- Ukraine
- D
- Franco-Belgian M
- Pilsen Brno
- Saar
- Lorraine x
- Krivoi Rog x
- Kerch x
- CRIMEA
- N. Spain
- B
- Massif Central
- oG oT oM
- Slovenia x
- G
- x
- K
- M
- Z
- B
- Elba x

Bituminous Coal
Lignite
x **Iron Ore**
T o **Industrial town largely dependent on hydro-electricity**

Map B: Europe: Major Cities and Very Densely Populated Regions

■ Towns with over 1m. inhabitants
• Towns with over 200 000 inhabitants

Very densely populated

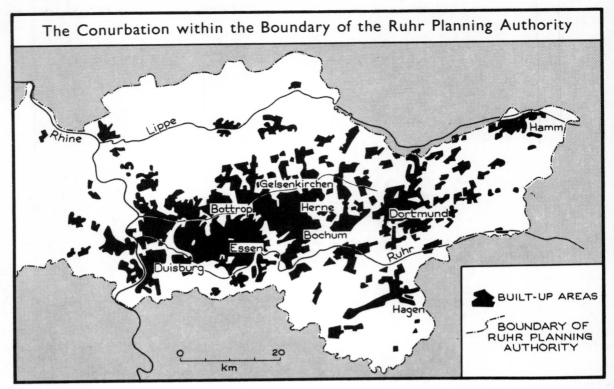

Map C

controlled the great Lorraine iron-ore field, the ore from which helped to build up the immensely important steel and heavy engineering industry of the Ruhr coal-mining area. The latter soon became one of the world's major industrial regions. After the First World War other European coalfields became centres of growing industries, especially in Poland, Czechoslovakia and European Russia. Map A on page 13 shows the four main coalfields concerned. Of these the Donbas was destined to become the principal heavy industrial region in the Soviet Union, using local coal and iron ore brought from Krivoi Rog and the Crimea.

Since the late 19th century new sources of power have become available. Electricity, mainly generated in coal-fired power stations and distributed by 'Grid' cables, allows factories to be sited more or less anywhere. In some countries, such as Switzerland, Italy, Norway and Sweden, running water is harnessed to generate hydro-electricity; specialized industries including electrical engineering, electro-chemicals and electro-smelting have grown up as a result as the cheap source of electrical power. Indeed northern Italy has become a major industrial region, and its prosperous modern cities attract a constant flood of destitute peasant migrants from the impoverished south of that country.

In certain parts of southern Europe, notably in Iberia and southern Italy, there are large conglomerations of people who derive their livelihood from semi-subsistence peasant farming, or from industries based largely on agricultural production. In many respects these peoples' lives are akin to those of the rural peasantry of Monsoon Asia: there is a similar economic backwardness coupled with the prevalence of ignorance, superstition and disease. Above all there is a similar relentless pressure of numbers on land resources, accompanied by a general sense of futility and fatalism. These clusters of dense population grew up on the coastlands of southern Europe largely because in that part of the Continent there is a great scarcity of flat, fertile land, and a rigorous summer drought due to the Mediterranean climate. Thus people settled where flattish land and water for irrigation were both available: here they developed a unique type of intensive irrigated polyculture on fertile *huertas* ('gardens').

14

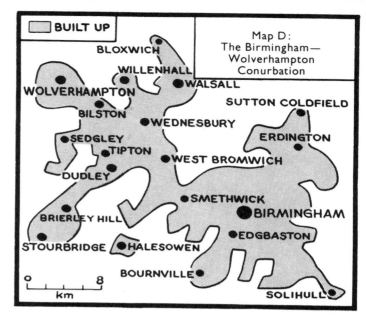

Map D:
The Birmingham—
Wolverhampton
Conurbation

Hemmed in by thousands of square miles of semi-desert, scrub and badlands runs a valley, seventeen miles long and about five wide, rich almost to the point of exaggeration. Steep, sharp mountains on one side seem to dive headlong into this valley to re-emerge on the other side. This is the *Huerta* (vegetable- and fruit-growing land) of the Spanish province of Murcia, in the middle of which stands the provincial capital, Murcia, shrouded with the sweet scent of orange blossom. Every inch of it is minutely cultivated with extreme care and hard work. There is an abundance of fruit trees, of almonds, figs, dates, oranges, apples, pears, pomegranates, quinces, grapefruit and, above all, lemons (largest production in Spain), not to mention other crops: corn, maize, cayenne pepper, olives and even rice, and many different vegetables; in fact, almost anything you could think of that is eaten by Europeans. Production is not limited to foodstuffs. 45 000 acres are used for cotton-growing. Four-fifths of the Spanish silk production comes from here, 2500 families have the special mulberry tree. . . .

Were it not for the River Segura this area would be desert . . . the sun, blazing down from a perpetually blue sky and reflected off the rocks of the badlands, knocks the temperature up to 114°F. now and again.[1]

Most of the peasants who work the *huertas* live in large, widely spaced villages so that the land looks strangely unoccupied despite its dense rural population. In addition to the villages most *huertas* include at least one large town, and in fact many such towns have extensive patches of irrigated farmland within their municipal boundaries. The map (*right*) shows the intermingling of urban and rural land in the Valencia *huerta*.

Yet another region of dense population is located in the eastern half of North America, especially in the north-east of the U.S.A. between Chicago and New York, and in the adjoining St. Lawrence Valley in Canada. This is essentially a modern industrial zone, in which the distribution of population correlates closely with the distribution of power resources, good transport routes and port facilities. In many respects, therefore, this thickly settled region of North America resembles the coalfield and port

[1] A. Rainey, *Geographical Magazine*.

conurbations of Europe. Compared with West and Central Europe, however, greater reliance is placed in North America on locally produced petroleum, natural gas and hydro-electricity. Even so, the major conurbations of North America lie in close proximity to the Appalachian Coalfield.

The only other considerable region of dense population in the world lies in Japan. This country shows a remarkable fusion of both densely populated rural and urban communities. Japanese peasant farmers, who constitute 45 per cent of the total population, practise a typical Monsoon Asian subsistence economy, whereas the millions of people living in vast industrial cities such as Tokyo (10 900 000) and Osaka (3 200 000) have much in common with their

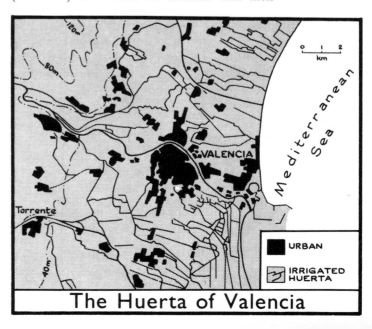

The Huerta of Valencia

The southern end of Manhattan Island, New York. Beyond the Hudson River lies Jersey City. The towering buildings of many Western cities permit a very high density of urban population. New York City has a population of more than 11 million and an average population density of about 9770 per square kilometre.

cities vitally dependent on electrical power and foreign trade.

In spite of her intensive farming and ever-growing industries Japan faces acute population pressures. After centuries of slow population growth, during which age-old methods of rice cultivation provided sufficient foodstuffs for the entire populace, Japan underwent a dramatic population 'explosion'. Between 1720 and 1840 total numbers remained constant at about 30 million, but since 1840 the total has shot up to 100 million, and is still increasing at 1·0 per cent per annum: at this rate it will double again within the next sixty years. With only one-seventh of their land surface cultivable the Japanese are faced with an acute problem of food supply.

For many years the *per capita* consumption of the staple food, rice, has been about $5\frac{1}{2}$ bushels, whilst the yield of Japanese paddy-fields is about 38 bushels per acre. The 7 000 000 acres under rice could thus support about 50 000 000 people, but the new acreage being brought under rice annually is only sufficient to support about one-quarter of the actual increase.[1]

Massive efforts to solve this dilemma have involved the deliberate expansion of industries, notably textiles and engineering, so that manufactured products can be traded overseas in return for foodstuffs and industrial raw materials. Japan has faced serious handicaps in her programme of industrialization, however, for the country has only limited resources of raw materials and, until recently, a comparatively small iron and steel industry. This map shows the densely packed manufacturing region and conurbation of the Tokyo Metropolitan Region.

The growth of very large urban settlements similar to those of Western Europe, North America and Japan has become one of the characteristics of human society in the mid-20th century. Until the 1930's the world's very large cities were almost entirely confined to economically advanced regions. Today, however, the populations of many underdeveloped countries are becoming urbanized at a rate of over 4 per cent p.a., so that their towns are doubling in size every 15 years. In Venezuela for example, the capital city of Caracas grew from 359 000 in 1941 to 1 764 000 in 1966 and other Venezuelan

counterparts in Europe and North America. By acquiring Western learning in science and technology the Japanese have built up huge industrial

[1] L. Dudley Stamp, *Asia*, Methuen, p. 640. (Very recently this problem has been eased by (i) a shift of taste away from rice eating by the Japanese public and (ii) the use of new mechanized methods of rice cultivation.)

The Tokyo Metropolitan Region

Maebashi & Takasaki
Utsunomiya
Ota & Oizumi
Mito & Katsuta
Oyama & Mamada
L. KASUMIGAURA
Kumagaya & Fukaya
Koga & Sowa
Kawagoe & Sayama
Tsuchiura & Ami
Omiya & Urawa
TOKYO
Chiba, Ichihara & Goi
TOKYO BAY
Kawasaki
Hiratsuka, Chigasaki & Fujisawa
Yokohama
PACIFIC OCEAN

0   60
km

BUILT-UP

Woomera, South Australia. This settlement of 5500 inhabitants owes its existence in the Australian desert entirely to the need for a remote rocket-testing location.

cities either equal or exceed this rate of growth. At the same time the Venezuelan farming population is also expanding rapidly at c. 11 per cent every decade, whilst the amount of cultivated land is actually decreasing. The result is that the Venezuelans are finding it progressively more difficult to feed not only their rapidly growing urban population but also the increasing numbers of people living in the countryside: in fact c. 87 people in Venezuela are trying to live from each square kilometre of cultivated land. This dilemma is being repeated nearly everywhere in the under-developed regions of the world, the problem being to expand agricultural production fast enough to accommodate the enormous simultaneous increase in numbers both on the farms and in the cities. (*See also pp.* 23–24).

So far we have considered only sizeable regions where population densities are high, and it has been shown that, generally speaking, these regions are located in parts of the world where geographical conditions favour intensive cultivation or the development of modern industries, or both of these activities. We shall next examine those regions which are very scantily peopled or are uninhabited. A comparison of the maps on page 10 with the world climate and relief maps in an atlas will indicate certain correlations. In particular notice that, almost without exception, the vast arid and semi-arid regions of the world contain few people.

Despite large-scale irrigation schemes (*see pages* 46–49) the deserts remain largely drought-stricken and forbidding wildernesses. There *are* exceptions, however, and one must beware of taking too deterministic a view of the influences of the physical environment on human affairs. The photo above and that on page 54 show examples of considerable settlements located right in the heart of hot deserts. The map overleaf shows the distribution of gold-mines in the West Australian Desert. At Kalgoorlie, for example, gold was discovered in 1892 and, despite the blistering heat and aridity of the

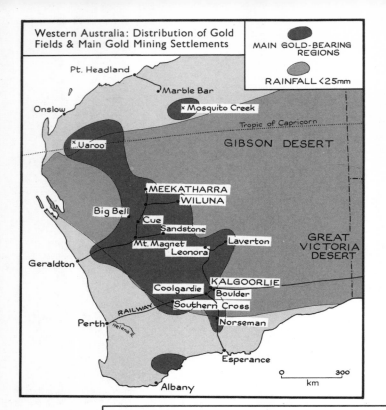

Western Australia: Distribution of Gold Fields & Main Gold Mining Settlements

MAIN GOLD-BEARING REGIONS

RAINFALL <25mm

Pt. Headland
Marble Bar
Onslow
x Mosquito Creek
Tropic of Capricorn
GIBSON DESERT
x Uaroo
MEEKATHARRA
WILUNA
Big Bell
Cue
Sandstone
Mt. Magnet
Leonora
Laverton
GREAT VICTORIA DESERT
Geraldton
Coolgardie
KALGOORLIE
Boulder
Southern Cross
RAILWAY
Norseman
Perth
Helena R.
Esperance
km
0 300
Albany

forestry. Examples include the timber and wood-pulp centres of Scandinavia, Quebec and north-west Russia and the important Russian ports of Murmansk and Archangel. Archangel (308 000) has exported skins and furs for nearly 400 years, but today it is best known as the principal lumber port of the Soviet Union. Throughout the summer logs are floated downstream to Archangel along the many headstreams and tributaries of the Northern Dvina. In Archangel the logs are handled by more than 150 sawmills and the timber products are shipped out via the White Sea in the following spring. Murmansk (279 000) is the largest town north of the Arctic Circle. It owes its importance (a) to its ice-free position and (b) to the growth of a large fishing fleet operating in the Barents Sea. Murmansk is linked to Moscow by rail and replaces Leningrad as the northern commercial port of the U.S.S.R. during the mid-winter freeze-up. In addition Murmansk is an important naval base and shipbuilding port and exports phosphates from the mines at nearby Kirovsk. (*See map below*).

COOL-GARDIE	°C	25	24	22	18	14	11	11	12	14	17	25	24
(417 m)	R.f. mm	10·2	17·8	15·2	15·2	33·0	30·5	22·9	22·9	15·2	17·8	12·7	15·2

whole region (see climate chart above), a township of 23 000 inhabitants rapidly came into being. Water is brought 564 kilometres to Kalgoorlie from the Mundaring Weir on the Helena River.

Another very scantily peopled region is the vast tundra- and taïga-covered lowland bordering the Arctic Ocean in North America and Eurasia. Cultivation in the tundra is virtually impossible due to the very short growing season (about two months) and the formation in summer of widespread swamps, for melt-water on the ground surface cannot drain through the permanently frozen subsoil. Although the taïga has a longer growing season—up to six months along its southern margins—the thin, infertile podzols do not favour cultivation and the region is still largely neglected by farmers.[1] As in the arid regions, however, there are certain 'oases' of relatively dense population in both tundra and taïga, mostly concerned with mining, trading or

[1] See, however, p. 69.

18

Position of Murmansk & Archangel

TUNDRA

TAÏGA

km
0 300

Barents Sea
Pechenga
Murmansk
KOLA
Kirovsk
PENINSULA
Kandalaksha
White Sea
Archangel
ARCTIC CIRCLE
N. Dvina
Kem
Belomorsk
U.S.S.R.
Karelia
L. Onega

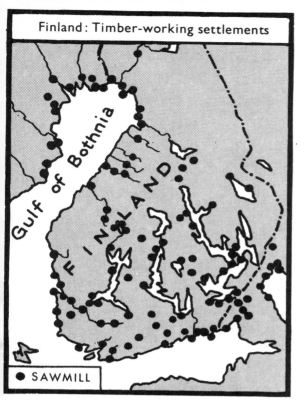

Finland: Timber-working settlements

Gulf of Bothnia

FINLAND

● SAWMILL

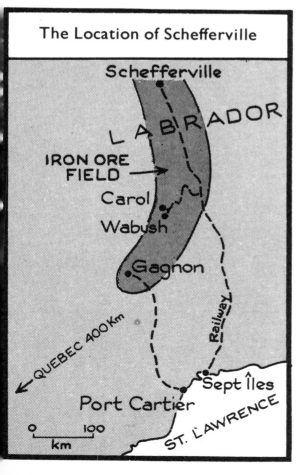

The Location of Schefferville

Schefferville

LABRADOR

IRON ORE FIELD →

Carol

Wabush

Gagnon

QUEBEC 400 Km

Railway

Sept Îles

Port Cartier

ST. LAWRENCE

0   100
km

There are many important mining centres, too, in the remote wilderness of northern Canada. One of the best known is Knob Lake (Schefferville) in Labrador. The following account of iron-mining there is characteristic of events now occurring at many locations in the Canadian Shield:

A few years ago no one lived within 200 miles of what is today the largest iron-mining operation in Canada. . . . The three great obstacles that prevented earlier exploitation of the area were the lack of any means of transporting the ore down to the St. Lawrence, the climate which limits the mining season to less than six months a year, and the difficulty of attracting labour to such an inhospitable spot. The transport difficulty was solved by the building, with the aid of an air lift, of the Quebec North Shore & Labrador Railway, which negotiates 356 miles of appalling country between Sept Îles and Knob Lake. (*Map below*). There were 17 ravines to be bridged, two mountains to be tunnelled under and tracts of muskeg to be defeated. Muskeg is Canada's Slough of Despond—a watery slush of moss two or three feet deep that floats on top of the permafrost, or permanently frozen ground, through which the water cannot penetrate. Today diesel locomotives haul trains of 125 ore cars each from Knob Lake to Sept Îles, whence the ore is shipped to Europe, the United States and other parts of Canada in less than 16 hours. The climate is still the master in the winter, when the ore, even if it could be got out of the ground, would freeze into immovable blocks in the cars. The Iron Ore Company of Canada and its associates which mine and ship the ore therefore concentrate everything on production during the summer. In the peak months of July, August and September the manager of operations at Schefferville has to get 100 000 tons of ore out of the ground every day or, one imagines, take up some other occupation.[2]

Tropical rain forests are also conspicuous (Maps, page 10) as regions containing relatively few inhabitants. Notable examples include Amazonia, parts of south-east Asia and the lower portions of the Congo Basin. These forests mostly occupy low-lying basins or coastal plains in low latitudes where the climate is very hot and very humid throughout the year. Although the natural vegetation is dense and luxuriant, soils are generally poor, due to the constant flushing out

[2] *The Times*, from a Special Correspondent.

19

of soluble mineral particles. Thus, even in areas where the dense forest cover has been removed, little systematic agriculture takes place and farming populations are thin and widely scattered. Other factors which hitherto have inhibited large-scale settlement in hot humid lands include the unhealthy and unpleasant climate, widespread swamps, hostility from primitive native inhabitants and remoteness from established world markets (*see also pages* 29–38). As in other sparsely settled regions, however, there are notable exceptions: in West Africa, for example, a combination of plantation tree cropping, subsistence cultivation and mining supports dense communities in southern Ghana and Nigeria. Elsewhere the exploitation of mineral wealth, often financed by European or North American concerns, explains the location of many isolated 'pockets' of population in the rain forests of Venezuela, Brazil, Central Africa, Malaysia and Indonesia.

A fourth category of scantily peopled lands includes the mountainous regions of the world. Here a combination of factors discourages settlement: most mountains and high altitude plateaus are characterized by cold, wet, bleak, infertile conditions, and are often virtually inaccessible. In addition there are considerable physiological obstacles to living at great heights.

Mountain sickness, the 'soroche' of the Andes, an unpleasant combination of splitting headaches, nausea, and, in bad cases, of bleeding from the nose and ears, affects people going up into high mountains, though the level at which it first occurs varies very much with the individual: some people begin to feel it after ascending only a few thousand feet, others not until they reach twelve or even fifteen thousand feet. But when living at these levels the worst effects generally soon pass off in healthy people, and in a few days they become partially acclimatised. At greater heights, however, acclimatisation gets more and more difficult, and at about twenty-five thousand feet there appears to be a critical zone where everything seems to change for the worse and the odds are all against even the best-trained mountaineer. Mountain sickness, and the great difficulty experienced in doing even very simple things at very high altitudes, is obviously a deterrent to permanent settlement. In both the Americas and in Central Asia the upper limit of settlement—not necessarily even permanent settle-ment, as much of it is during the summer only —is at about 16 000 to 17 000 feet.[1]

Even so, there is a fairly dense population of semi-nomadic herdsmen living at 11–12 000 feet on the arid plateaus of Bolivia and Tibet and there are notable high-altitude cities at La Paz (150 000 people at 12 000 feet), Lhasa (20 000 people at 11 800 feet) and Shigatze (14 000 people at 12 000 feet).

Many mining settlements in the Andes are higher than this: the workmen at the sulphur mine of Aucanquilcha in Chile, itself at 18 800 feet, live at 17 500 feet and begin their day's work by walking up 1300 feet through sand and powdered sulphur; when in the mine they can do as much work as the ordinary man can do at sea-level, and after a hard day's work will spend an evening at 17 500 feet practising football.[1]

These exceptions show once again that Man is capable of overcoming formidable obstacles to settlement if it is economically advantageous to do so.

Any analysis of the world distribution of population must take into account the factor of *migration*. Large-scale movements of peoples across both land and sea have been common-place throughout the entire history of Man. Some authorities, notably Professor Griffith Taylor[2], seek to explain the present distribution of races[3] as the result of successive migrations of peoples from a common 'heartland', or place of origin, in Central Asia. The main details of this hypo-thesis are summarized in the notes on the map (*right*): remember that the migrations indicated there took place throughout tens of thousands of years and involved relatively few people. Much more significant, in terms of the present distribu-tion and density of world population, are the migrations which have occurred during the past

[1] M. S. Anderson, *Geography of Living Things*, E.U.P.
[2] See *Geography of the Twentieth Century*, ed. Taylor. Methuen.
[3] *Race* is a biological term. The human species may be sub-divided, on the basis of differing physical characteristics, into three main groups, viz. the *Negroids* (with woolly hair and broad noses), the *Caucasians* (with wavy hair and narrow noses) and the *Mongoloids* (with lank, straight hair and noses of intermediate width). The principal distinguishing features determining an individual's race are the nature and colour of his hair, colour of eyes and skin and shape of head. In spite of many assertions to the contrary there is no convincing evidence that there are any significant variations in intelli-gence or ability to learn between the various races of man-kind. Any claims for the existence of a 'Master Race', as put forward for example by the Nazis in pre-war Germany, are dangerous nonsense.

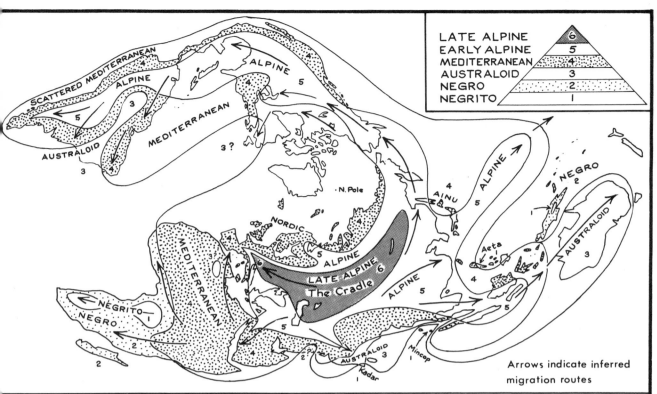

LATE ALPINE 6
EARLY ALPINE 5
MEDITERRANEAN 4
AUSTRALOID 3
NEGRO 2
NEGRITO 1

Arrows indicate inferred migration routes

Distribution of Major Races at the Beginning of the Christian Era

Professor Griffith Taylor endeavoured to show that the directions of early human migrations were determined in part by the natural geographical corridors of the various continents. Professor Taylor asserted that there are representatives of the five major races (Alpine, Mediterranean, Australoid, Negro and Negrito) in each of the continents (see map). He also suggested[4] that right up to the 16th century Great Age of Discovery, migrations from south-central Asia were the key to the distribution of races. This theory needs re-evaluation in the light of recent discoveries of traces of very early Man in East Africa. Possibly Man evolved simultaneously from simian stock in various 'cradles' in separate continents.

400 years, i.e. since the Great Age of Discovery. These migrations have mainly involved Europeans, for the world's oceans were first effectively opened up as a result of the remarkable voyages of West European explorers and merchants. The present distribution of white settlement in the Americas, Africa and Australasia is largely attributable to these early voyages, the exact direction of many of which was often quite fortuitous.

The most significant migration of non-European peoples in recent history was the enforced movement of tens of millions of African Negroes to the Americas during the notorious

Slave Trade of the 18th century. The large Negro populations of the U.S.A., Central America, the West Indies and Brazil consist of descendants of these slaves. Much smaller numbers of Indians were also moved to South and East Africa and the West Indies as indentured labourers. In addition there have been sizeable movements of Asians within Asia, nearly 2 million Japanese migrating to the adjacent mainland and islands and some 10 million Indians and 20 million Chinese settling mostly in the south-eastern part of the continent.

Can migration significantly relieve the pressure of people on the land in those parts of the world where living standards are below par? Generally speaking the answer is no, because:

1. The number of people involved is too great. In India alone it would be necessary to tranship some 13 million people *annually* merely to keep the population stabilized at its present total. The shipment, rehousing and resettlement of such very large numbers of people would entail virtually insoluble administrative problems.

2. There are no large regions of potentially

[4] For further details see Ch. XIV, Griffith Taylor, op. cit.

prosperous farmland to which millions of subsistence farmers can be moved. Most regions of the world favourable to agriculture have already been settled, the effective limits of ready cultivation having been reached in all continents.

3. There are serious political hindrances to the free international movement of peoples. Most states severely restrict immigration, permitting entry only to those migrants who can readily be absorbed into productive employment. In addition most advanced white communities have regulations designed to keep out coloured people: this is to avoid social and economic problems arising from the operation of a 'colour bar'.

4. The costs of emigration are high, and most would-be migrants have very little money—indeed this is one of the main reasons why they wish to emigrate.

The question also arises whether it is possible to stipulate a total population which would best suit a particular country. In other words is it possible to state that a country is underpopulated, overpopulated, or has an optimum number of people? On economic grounds a country can be said to have an *optimum population* if an addition or subtraction of numbers would lead to a significant decrease in the community's material well-being. It should be noted that the concept of an optimum population is essentially dynamic, any stipulated figure being calculated on the basis of a country's existing technology. Technological know-how is all-important in this respect, for any improvements in the methods of producing, distributing and exchanging commodities may make it possible for a country to sustain a larger population at a higher level of living. As a *rough* guide to illustrate this principle the following 'equation' is useful:

$$\text{Level of living} = \frac{\text{Natural resources} \times \text{Technique}}{\text{Population}}$$

A country's natural resources, i.e. its reserves of minerals, fuels, soils, forests and so on, are more or less given, but their availability and value can be greatly increased by improvements in technique. A simple example of this can be given from the mining industry: improvements in methods of extracting metals from mineral ores have made it economically worthwhile to re-work waste-tips of Cornish tin and copper ores. Similarly, new methods of mechanized cultivation and fertilizing have greatly improved the yields of soils on the chalklands of Britain. A little reflection will bring to mind similar examples in which improvements in the technology of manufacturing industry, fishing, forestry, agriculture and communications have led to greater material abundance being obtained from given resources. Where, as in the U.S.A. and Western Europe and the U.S.S.R., such new techniques as computer calculating and automation are being applied, any stipulated optimum population must be treated with added caution.

However, with these reservations in mind, there is general agreement that parts of such countries as India, China and Brazil are grossly overpopulated, a situation made tragically evident by the existence of widespread and endemic famine, disease and poverty. The best example of an *under*populated country is Canada, where the government considers that the existing population of 20 million could profitably be doubled by the end of this century. Vast regions of mineral-rich northern Canada await development and there are still enormous resources of untapped hydro-electricity. Australians are also anxious to increase their total population, but the scope for future development there is less than in Canada, for much of Australia consists of desert and semi-desert. The situation is complicated, too, by a 'White Australia' policy, whereby coloured immigrants are prevented from taking up permanent residence. It is feared that an 'open door' policy would lead to the immigration into tropical Australia of millions of Asiatic subsistence cultivators who would prove difficult to assimilate into the country's political and social life. Furthermore by accepting low wage rates such immigrants might endanger existing living standards. On the other hand the Australian government gives generous economic aid to white would-be immigrants who are healthy, skilled and adaptable. It is hoped to increase Australia's present population of 11·5 million to 20 million by the year 2000.

In the case of both Canada and Australia it should be noted that the aim is to increase greatly the density of population. This illustrates the point that a high *density* of population does not necessarily entail *over*population. Some industrial regions of Great Britain have population densities greatly exceeding those of rural India, but there are no economic grounds for regarding Great Britain as being overpopulated.

On the other hand the drought-stricken North-east region of Brazil, with a population density of less than 2 per square kilometre, is notorious for its poverty and hunger and is a classic example of overpopulation. However, a people might be content with their lot even though their level of living falls well below the minimum which Western man regards as tolerable: one should hesitate before applying one's own standards to an alien culture.

3. The problem of world population and food supply

In 1798 Thomas Malthus published his famous *Essay on the Principle of Population*, a work which focused public attention for the first time on problems of food supply arising from a rapidly increasing population. The essence of the Malthusian doctrine, in Malthus's own words, is that

> the power of population is indefinitely greater than the power in the earth to provide a subsistence for man.

Malthus suggested that whereas population increases in geometrical progression, supplies of foodstuffs increase in arithmetical progression. This assumption is not in fact very accurate, but it does indicate certain basic trends in 'backward' societies. Assuming that, to begin with, food supply could be doubled after twenty years, this means that within a century the supply of food would increase *six times*: meanwhile the population would have multiplied *thirty-two times*, as the following table shows:

Years	0	20	40	60	80	100
Unit of food	1	2	3	4	5	6
Unit of population	1	2	4	8	16	32

This hypothesis implies that mankind is faced with the dismal prospect of never being able to solve the problem of famine. The amount of food available per head of population would fall until numbers become checked by such 'natural' disasters as famine, disease and war. In Great Britain, where his views at first caused great concern, the predictions of Malthus were not realized because of the unprecedented and unforeseen increases in productivity during the 19th and 20th centuries, increases largely due to technological improvements in industry, agriculture and transport. These improvements helped make it possible for Britain's population to rise from 10 million in 1801 to 37 million in 1901 and still enjoy a much improved standard of living. Another reason was that modern industrial Britain was able to obtain great quantities of cheap foodstuffs and industrial raw materials from overseas, in return for exports of manufactured goods. Furthermore, the rate of increase of population in Great Britain slackened off considerably in the early 20th century (*Chart B, page* 2), for the reasons discussed in the last chapter. Such ameliorating factors do not apply, however, to all peoples undergoing a population explosion, and today very large numbers of people in underdeveloped parts of the world face a grim Malthusian dilemma. The maps overleaf illustrate the unsatisfactory food situation in Africa, India, Pakistan and South-east Asia, and Latin America as compared with that in the advanced economic regions. Further evidence of unsatisfactory diets in many underdeveloped regions is given in Tables 2 & 3 overleaf.

The calories referred to in Table 2 show the amount of heat energy obtained from foodstuffs when they are burned in a calorimeter. A calorie is defined as the amount of heat needed to raise the temperature of 1000 grammes of water by 1°C. from 15° to 16°C. Most experts agree that a daily intake of about 3000 calories is adequate, whereas an intake of less than 2000 calories per day is most unsatisfactory.[1] The optimum calorific intake varies somewhat according to a person's way of life and the climate in which he lives. Generally speaking people in cold temperate regions need more calories per day than those in hot, tropical lands. Several experts[2] suggest that in most developing regions each person needs at least 2400 calories per day. According to Table 2, therefore, some 70 per cent of the world's

[1] See, however, note at foot of page 24, overleaf.
[2] See, e.g., L. Dudley Stamp, *Our Developing World*, Faber, p. 68.

Table 2

CONTRASTS IN NUTRITION BETWEEN ECONOMICALLY UNDERDEVELOPED AND ECONOMICALLY DEVELOPED REGIONS[1]

Item	Economically under-developed regions[2]	Economically developed regions[3]
Calories (per person per day)	2150	3060
Total protein (grammes per person per day)	58	90
Animal protein (grammes per person per day)	9	44
Population (U.N. estimates for 1969)	c. 2500 million	c. 1000 million

[1] Freedom from Hunger Campaign, Basic Study No. 10, F.A.O., p. 14.
[2] Far East, Near East, Africa, Latin America.
[3] Europe, U.S.S.R., Anglo-America, Argentina, Uruguay, Australasia.

Table 3

CONSUMPTION OF ANIMAL PROTEIN

(per person per day)

New Zealand	74·8 g	Good diet
Uruguay	61·9	
United Kingdom	53·4	
Austria	47·5	
Israel	36·3	
Chile	29·2	Moderate to poor diet
Spain	23·4	
Mexico	23·4	
Japan	16·9	
Egypt	12·2	Very poor diet
Guatemala	8·5	
Pakistan	7·7	
India	5·9	

The *quality* of foodstuffs is as important as the *quantity*, and a proper balance should be kept between the consumption of carbohydrates (found, for example, in cereals and potatoes), proteins and fats. Proteins can be obtained from vegetable sources such as soya beans, pulses, nuts and oil-seeds, and from animal foods such as meat, fish, eggs and dairy produce. Proteins are especially valuable in promoting good health, each person needing at least 70 grammes per day, of which 20 grammes should come from animal sources. Note the highly unsatisfactory intakes of animal protein in certain of the countries listed in Table 3. The diets of tropical peoples also tend to lack important vitamins and minerals such as phosphorus, calcium, iodine, sodium and iron. These minerals are normally absorbed through salts, but salts are deficient in tropical soils due to excessive leaching (*see also page* 29). The craving for salt is sometimes so strong among tropical peoples that they attempt to assuage it by eating soil—a practice called geophagy.

Sometimes dietary deficiencies are a result of customs, habit, tastes and taboos which restrict the range of food consumed: milk, for example, is believed by some inhabitants of Grenada to

population never get enough to eat.[4] In such regions, too, the inadequacy of diet is especially marked at the end of the agricultural year, when stocks of food are running out. Near-famine conditions therefore tend to recur at the busiest time of year, with the result that work is often skimped and inefficient—with resulting lower crop yields—because of hunger and the apathy which hunger generates.

[4] It should be noted that the physiology of nutrition is still a very inexact science. For example, one eminent authority —Dr. Colin Clark—puts the minimum calorie requirement of an Asian population '. . . within the range 1600–2000 per person per day, depending on body weight, temperature and the amount of agricultural work done' (Colin Clark, 'Is the World Starving?' *Daily Telegraph*, December 1967). If this estimate is correct it means that the number of permanently hungry people in the world is relatively few. The fact still remains, however, that hunger and malnutrition are widespread in certain regions, notably in underdeveloped countries such as Brazil, China and India, where '. . . medical surveys find nearly 20 per cent of the children showing clear signs of protein deficiency, and there is considerable actual

hunger as well' (ibid.). Other authorities take a very much bleaker view of the world food situation. According to Professor René Dumont, the French agronomist who is director of research at the Institut National Agronomique in Paris '. . . The world will face the greatest famine in history by about 1980 . . . World population is year by year out-stripping food production. Throughout the Third World, since 1959, population increase has been 26 per 1000 per year and food production has increased for only 15 to 20 people per 1000 per year. There are others who go further than I do and say that it's too late to avoid the terrible catastrophe and that it could come as soon as 1975.' (Professor Dumont, in a speech at the Africa Centre, as reported in the *Observer*, December 1967.)

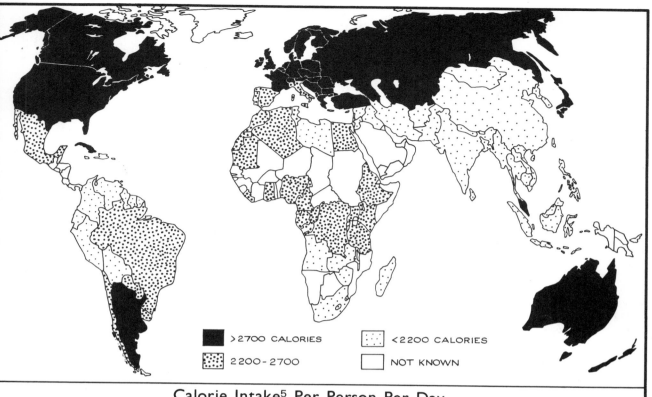

Calorie Intake[5] Per Person Per Day

■ >2700 CALORIES	⋮ <2200 CALORIES
▪ 2200-2700	□ NOT KNOWN

[5] Based on estimates supplied by F.A.O.

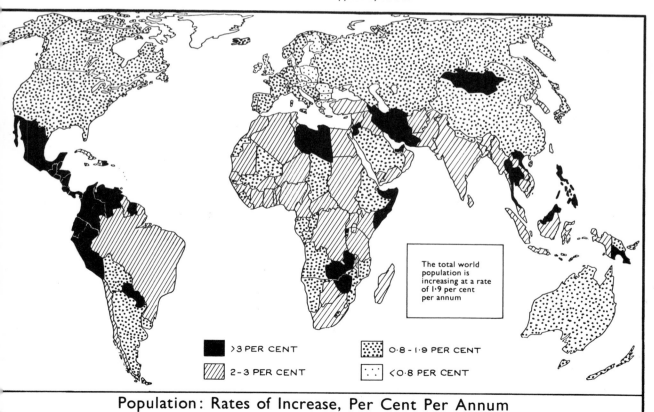

The total world population is increasing at a rate of 1·9 per cent per annum

■ >3 PER CENT	⋮ 0·8-1·9 PER CENT
▨ 2-3 PER CENT	⋯ <0·8 PER CENT

Population: Rates of Increase, Per Cent Per Annum

Source: U.N. Demographic Yearbook, 1967.

(Top) *India's 'holy cows' wander where they will in the cities, unharmed and unmolested.*

(Bottom) *Children in Mysore search garbage cans for food, while two boys tussle for possession of a piece of edible refuse. There are an estimated 150 million cattle in India, apart from buffaloes. These cattle could help relieve starvation, but the slaughter of cows is forbidden as they are sacred symbols of motherhood to millions of Hindus.*

give children worms, while the Sinhalese attribute many diseases to this valuable animal protein.[1] Hindus are forbidden on religious grounds from eating cow's meat and orthodox Jews will not eat pork. Amongst the Masai herdsmen of East Africa

meat and milk may never be eaten on the same day, nor may they be allowed to come into

1 Pierre Gourou, *The Tropical World*, Longmans, p. 72. This book is an indispensable source of reference in studying the human geography of tropical lands.

any contact with one another. The infringement of this rule would, it is believed, cause serious disease among the cattle.[2]

Solomon Islanders forbid their women from fishing and some fish are forbidden them as food, whilst certain Eskimo tribes do not cook or eat caribou meat in an igloo for fear of offending Sedna, the goddess of seals and walruses. Improvements in diet among such peoples must obviously go hand in hand with education. To a certain extent, too, the potential nutritional value of foodstuffs is wasted by slow and inefficient cooking techniques. (*See also p.* 28).

The main problem, however, lies in sheer lack of quantity in those underdeveloped regions of the world where tremendous increases in population are predicted for the immediate future.

If food production were to increase at only the same rate as population over this period [i.e. up to 2000] we should not be able to provide

2 C. Daryll Forde, *Habitat Economy and Society*, Methuen, p. 297.

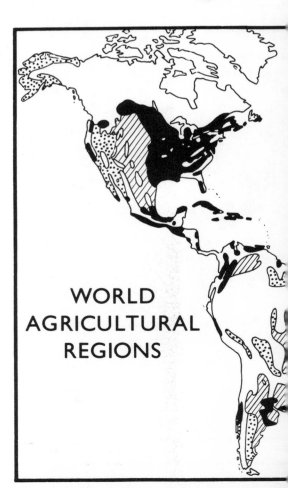

WORLD AGRICULTURAL REGIONS

the rising generation with the improvements in diet which have now become a part of the aspiration of hundreds of millions of people throughout the world.[3]

In fact it has been calculated that, to provide an adequate balanced diet of 2400 calories, including 20 grammes of animal protein per person per day, food supplies must be multiplied by four in Asia and the Far East, by three to four in Latin America, by three in the Near East and by two to three in Africa.[4]

This map shows those parts of the world which are at present cultivated: they amount to approximately 10 per cent of the land surface of the globe and cover an area of approximately 1753 million hectares. With a present world population of 3400 million, this works out at roughly 0·5 hectare per person. Bearing in mind that on average it takes just over 0·4 hectare of cultivated land to feed one person, that the area under crops in any one year is much less than the cultivable area and that the world population is increasing by some 65 million every year, it is obvious that humanity is pressing heavily on present soil resources. To what extent can this pressure be eased by bringing fresh land under the plough? Experts vary widely in their estimates, but Professor Sir Dudley Stamp suggested[5] that a further 20 per cent of the land surface of the globe is cultivable. This figure is arrived at as follows:

Proportion of world's land surface:

Too cold for cultivation	one-fifth
Too arid for cultivation	one-fifth
Too mountainous for cultivation	one-fifth
Without soil (i.e. bare rock)	one-tenth
Already cultivated	one-tenth
Remaining to be brought under cultivation	**one-fifth**

[3] P. V. Sukhatme, *Journal of the Royal Statistical Society, Series A (General)*, vol. 124.
[4] P. V. Sukhatme, loc. cit.

[5] L. Dudley Stamp, op. cit.

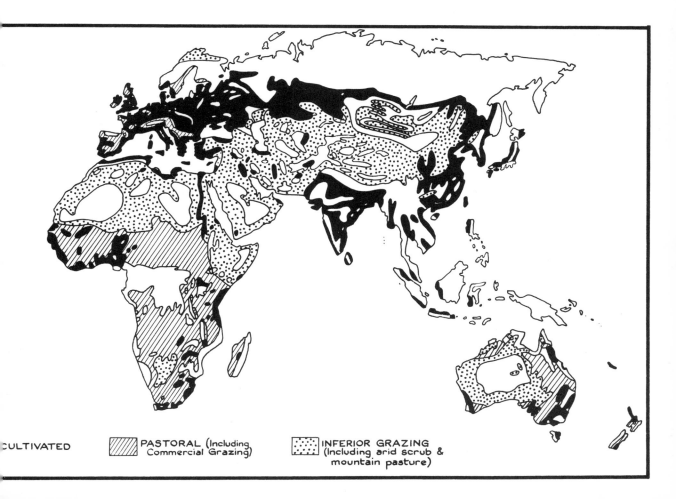

CULTIVATED   PASTORAL (Including Commercial Grazing)   INFERIOR GRAZING (Including arid scrub & mountain pasture)

The areas offering the best opportunities for agricultural expansion fall into four geographical regions, as follows: (i) equatorial lands, (ii) savanas, (iii) arid lands and (iv) humid temperate lands. Each of these regions will now be considered in turn.

Fulani women preparing a meal in Nigeria. Such laborious and often inefficient methods of cooking waste time and may reduce the nutritive benefits of foodstuffs.

Section 2. Possibilities of extending world agriculture

4. The equatorial lands

Equatorial Lands include huge areas which are at present completely undeveloped and largely un-inhabited, whilst much of the remainder is under-developed and only scantily peopled. These are the great rain-forest regions of the globe (*Map, p. 10*) within which development is hindered mainly by a hot, humid climate. The climate in all Equatorial lowlands is in fact remarkably constant: temperatures rarely fall much below 21°C. or rise much above 32°C.; mean daily temperatures hover for long periods around 27°C. and a heavy rainfall is well distributed throughout the year. Torrential convectional rain falls on most days, usually in the afternoon following the build-up of huge formations of cumulonimbus clouds.

> On most days . . . a heavy shower would fall some time in the afternoon, producing a most welcome coolness. The approach of the rain-clouds was after a uniform fashion very interesting to observe. First, the cool sea-breeze, which commenced to blow about 10 o'clock, and which had increased in force with the increasing power of the sun, would flag and finally die away. The heat and electric tension of the atmosphere would then become almost insupportable. Languor and uneasiness would seize on everyone; even the denizens of the forest betraying it by their motions. White clouds would appear in the east and gather into cumuli, with an increasing blackness along their lower portions. The whole eastern horizon would become almost suddenly black, and this would spread upwards, the sun at length becoming obscured. Then the rush of a mighty wind is heard through the forest, swaying the tree-tops; a vivid flash of lightning bursts forth, then a crash of thunder, and down streams the deluging rain.[1]

[1] H. W. Bates, *The Naturalist on the Amazons*, John Murray.

It is this deluging rain which produces the major snag in the agricultural development of rain-forest regions—**leached soils**. Rain water accumulates on the ground much faster than it can be evaporated, absorbed by plant roots or drained off by rivulets and streams. Hence there is a constant downward seepage of warm water which dissolves away great quantities of valuable plant nutrients, e.g. nitrates, phosphates, potash and even silicates. The virtually worthless soil which remains is called a **laterite**. Laterites are also markedly deficient in humus, for fallen leaves and twigs oxidize very rapidly in the steamy heat and decomposition is accelerated by the activities of countless termites and bacteria. Hence Equatorial soils contain only about 1·8 per cent humus whereas the figure for many temperate soils is over 10 per cent. The leaching effect of Equatorial rain-storms is greatly accentuated if the forest cover is removed. This is because deforestation results in a dramatic rise in soil temperatures,[2] which in turn greatly increases both the solvent action of rain water and the rate of decay of organic waste. Moreover, the felling of trees adds to the amount of water on the ground, for the 'umbrella' effect of the vegetation is removed and no water is absorbed by tree roots.

In spite of these mineral and humus deficiencies the Equatorial lowlands, in their virgin state, are clothed in a dense and luxuriant forest vegetation. The maintenance of this proliferation of trees depands, however, on a delicate natural equilibrium: just enough fresh humus constantly becomes available to enable existing trees to survive and new plants to replace those which have decayed. Once the forest is cleared, how-ever, and the underlying sandy laterite is exposed to the full impact of the rains, forest may

[2] Prof. Gourou op. cit. quotes the following figures: 77°–79°F. with forest cover; 104°F. following deforestation.

have the greatest difficulty in re-establishing itself. A notable example of this is the cutover region of Trinidad, where deforested areas abandoned to nature develop a secondary growth of brushwood.

Agricultural production in Equatorial rainforest regions has hitherto been achieved by three main methods: (i) shifting cultivation; (ii) plantation cropping and (iii) padi-rice cultivation. Primitive forms of **shifting cultivation** (*ladang*) are traditional in most rain forests, being practised, for example, by peoples as widely separated as the Boro of western Amazonia, the Yoruba and Boloki of the African forests and the Kuoys of northern Cambodia. The photos show both traditional and modern mechanized methods of clearing and cultivating forested land in West Africa.

Once the land has been cleared it is possible to grow crops such as maize, yams, rice, sago, tapioca and groundnuts. For the first few years yields are satisfactory, partly due to the presence in the soil of wood-ash derived from the burnt vegetation. But soil fertility soon fades and thereafter it becomes necessary to apply great quantities of manure, compost and expensive mineral fertilizers. Leaching is so strong that a top dressing of manure which in temperate latitudes would suffice for two to three years lasts for only a few months on rain-forest soils. The sowing of food crops also reacts unfavourably on the quantity of humus retained in the soil.

Research has shown in fact that the protection of the humus in the soil requires the maintenance of a certain relation between the nitrogen and carbon. It would therefore be less necessary to give the soil organic nitrogen, in the form of green manure for instance, than to keep in the earth an adequate quantity of woody matter which will decompose slowly and secure a supply of carbon over a long period, thus allowing a considerable amount of nitrogen to be kept. The forest yields this woody matter, but dry food crops do not. Hence, it is not surprising to know that such crops waste more than ten times the mineral substances they consume and that recently cleared land may lose up to nearly 900 lb. of nitrogen per acre every year.[1]

Some shifting cultivators delay soil exhaustion by employing a system of rotation. In Nigeria,

for example, the Tivs plant a main crop of yams the first year, millet the second and sesame the third, as well as supplementary crops of water melons, sweet potatoes, beans, *voandzu*, hibisci and cassava. Within a short space of time, however, all cultivators must move on, for the soil steadily loses its goodness and a mounting growth of weeds hinders cultivation. Attempts to crop the land for more than about five years may so exhaust the ground that forest vegetation cannot re-establish itself and this will delay the natural recovery of the soil during its fallow period. It takes from eight to twelve years for trees to reclothe an abandoned rain-forest clearing and a further twenty years for sufficient humus to collect to enable the land to be brought safely back into cultivation. Such methods of farming obviously call for enormous areas of forest to feed relatively very few people: in Sumatra, for example, *ladang* supports only about thirty persons to the square mile (11·5 to the square kilometre). In Zambia, amongst the Lala people, the figure is even lower. The Lala live on the forest-covered Serenje Plateau, where each family destroys about 7·3 hectares of forest and piles the debris on a further 0·5 hectares of land. About 60 per cent of the total land surface is cultivable and the fallow period lasts for twenty-two years. As there are 6·7 persons to each family the land is therefore capable of supporting 2·3 persons per square kilometre.[2] Attempts to accommodate greater numbers in a *ladang* system by shortening the fallow period lead to the replacement of tree growth by coarse grasses, thus opening up the ground to soil erosion. It is clear that shifting cultivation offers no solution to the problem of mounting population pressures on land resources in underdeveloped tropical lands.

Plantation agriculture is, generally speaking, a very much more efficient and productive method of exploiting the agricultural potential of rain-forest regions. Plantations are large tropical farms which usually concentrate on producing one main cash crop, although subsidiary cash and subsistence crops may be grown as well. Most plantations were developed in the 18th and 19th centuries by European or North American merchants and many are still owned by or have close commercial links with large 'Western'

[1] Gourou, op. cit. (1st edn., p. 30).

[2] See M. D. U. Peeters, *Land Usage in Serenje District, Rhodesia*, Livingston Paper No. 19, Oxford, 1950.

business corporations, e.g. Fyffes (bananas), Dunlop and Ford (rubber) and Cadbury (cacao). With the exception of Australia, however, the labour force on plantations consists entirely of non-whites.

A well-organized plantation is able to avoid the depletion of soils which makes shifting cultivation such an unsatisfactory system of farming. This is achieved by concentrating on the production of tree crops, so that an 'umbrella' of vegetation is maintained between the soil and the hot sun and heavy rainfall. Even so, there are dangers, for reckless clearing will cause a dangerous increase in run-off, which in turn entails soil leaching and erosion, as well as flooding and swamp conditions in valleys and on lower hill slopes. These hazards are avoided by

The clearing and cultivation of rain-forest soils is an arduous and labour-consuming task when done by hand. Yet handhoeing such as is shown (right) *is in some respects preferable to large-scale mechanized methods* (below), *for wholesale disturbance of the ground may accentuate the dangers of soil erosion during the frequent heavy rainstorms.*

the *gradual* substitution of tree crops such as rubber, cacao, oil-palm and bananas for the natural forest vegetation. Of these the oil-palm does less damage to the soil than any other, although this palm needs a great deal of mineral food (350 kg per ha, as compared with 120 kg for coffee and 59 kg for rubber trees). In addition the ground between the planted trees is protected by shrubs, bushes, creepers and shade-tolerant food crops such as legumes and yams. As well as binding and sheltering the soil, some of these plants, e.g. deep-rooted shrubs, bring back leached minerals to the surface and make them available as plant nutrients. The ground-cover of shrubs also helps maintain a steady return of woody matter and humus to the soil. Additional precautions to prevent soil leaching and erosion include the application of large quantities of mineral fertilizers and compost, as well as the construction of contour ditches, terraces and emergency flood drains.

Enlightened plantation methods such as these are now standard practice, but in many parts of the world they have only become so in recent years. Very large areas of rain-forest soils were formerly destroyed by unsatisfactory farming methods, notably in Brazil and the Caribbean Islands. 'Get-rich-quick' pioneer settlers deforested huge patches of land, planted tobacco or sugar-cane or cotton without any thought for soil conservation, and later abandoned the plantations when fertility was exhausted. The folly of this short-term approach is now recognized and generally guarded against by government control. In some cases plantation owners caused serious damage quite unwittingly by ploughing their land in European style. The plough is now highly suspect in tropical lands, as the disturbance of the soil which its use involves appears often to precipitate erosion. Many authorities deprecate its use and urge careful hand planting of both tree crops and cover vegetation.

Padi-rice cultivation requires high temperatures, abundant moisture and sunshine, and flourishes best on swampy ground. Hitherto its cultivation in rain-forest regions has largely been confined to the peninsulas and islands of South-East Asia, notably in Indo-China and Java, amongst peoples following traditional methods of farming evolved in Monsoon conditions. Success-

Coconut plantation on the Windward coast of St. Vincent, West Indies.

Hand-planting of rice in an Indian padi-field.

ful cultivation along these lines calls for an enormous supply of human labour, up to 620 man/work days a year per hectare where two successive rice crops are grown. All aspects of padi growing—ditch-digging, preparing seedbeds ploughing, smoothing the mud, planting, manuring, weeding and so on—receive careful and expert attention. Hence yields are high and the farmlands can support a dense population and favour the progress of civilization.

The constant addition of compost and manure and of river silt during each controlled flooding keep the land highly fertile, even though there is no fallow period: many padi-fields in South-east Asia have been yielding good rice crops annually for over 4000 years. Submergence beneath carefully regulated flood waters also protects the soil from erosion. The system whereby seedlings are raised in nursery beds before being planted out allows great economy in land use: no sooner is one crop harvested than a new batch of strong young plants is transplanted from the seedbed.

An extraordinary network of ponds, canals and ditches ensures that water for irrigation is available throughout the year. Padi-rice regions are also remarkably free from malaria, although this disease is often found in tropical swamps. This is because the larvae of the dangerous *Anopheles* mosquito do not like the mostly muddy and stagnant waters found in irrigation ponds and padi-fields, and are repelled by the presence of manure and compost. Where rice cultivation depends on *running* water, as in the terraced hill-slopes of Java, malaria *is* a serious problem, but the disease is gradually being brought under control by spraying DDT.

Oriental methods have not been widely adopted in other physically comparable regions mainly because of the huge labour requirements involved. This is despite the fact that padi-rice growing offers by far the best way of producing carbohydrates in a rain-forest environment. Native African rice (*Oryza glaberrina*) is inferior, but that introduced from Asia (*Oryza sativa*) gives good yields along the swamp coasts of both West and East Africa. In both these regions padi-

33

rice supports dense 'refugee' populations who sought sanctuary in remote lowland swamps from tribal warfare farther inland. These peoples adopted intensive rice cultivation of necessity, as the only means of supporting themselves in congested farming conditions. Padi-rice also supports dense rural populations among the Merina people of Madagascar, where the crop was introduced from Indonesia. Outside Africa two widely separated experiments in padi-rice production are noteworthy. At Belém, in Amazonia, the Brazilian Instituto Agrônomique do Norte has obtained good yields from flooded alluvial areas. In north-west Australia Territory Rice Ltd. has large experimental farms in the Tortilla Flats region.[1] Rice seeds are sown from the air by low-flying aircraft and the harvest is reaped by crawler tractors. In 1966 some 500 000 tonnes of high-quality rice were obtained and a similar experimental scheme is located in the Ord River Valley in North Kimberley (*see Map.*)

It seems clear that huge areas of rain-forest now lying virtually untouched could be made economically productive. To achieve this it will first be necessary to make such remote regions as Amazonia, the inner Congo Basin and central Borneo and New Guinea more readily accessible. Improved road and rail links, for example, between the coastal and interior regions of Peru, Columbia and Ecuador would make feasible the effective colonization of a vast zone along the eastern slopes of the Andes. Real economic advance will only be achieved when the wasteful,

dangerous and unproductive systems of *ladang* are replaced by more scientific farming methods. Plantation and padi-rice techniques, adapted to suit precise local conditions, seem to offer the best solutions. In Malaya, for example, rubber trees are grown both on large plantations and side by side with food crops on small subsistence plots, thus providing peasants with a steady cash income. Similar conditions apply in West Africa as regards cacao production, for

... most of the forest region of Ghana... consists of a mosaic of cocoa plantations, food farms, and secondary regrowth. The cocoa-trees are not planted in orderly rows but in scattered patches of a few acres, under the shade of large forest trees, with crops like yams, plantains, and peppers growing along-side and dense tangles of young trees and creepers engulfing recently farmed plots.[2]

The Cocoa Research Station at Tafo conducts experiments with insecticides, new strains and fertilizers, and Government agencies make great efforts to spread knowledge of new ideas for improving yields. Fitzgerald[3] reckons that the food resources of Sierra Leone, Liberia and the Ivory Coast could be greatly expanded by a fuller use of methods such as these. In particular he suggests that the production of palm-oil from the Ivory Coast could easily be expanded by at least *twenty-five* times from the present output of about 8000 tonnes p.a. Yet another

[1] See R. G. Golledge, Agricultural Experiments in North-western Australia, *Geography*, No. 215.

[2] A. T. Grove, *Africa South of the Sahara*, O.U.P., p. 117.
[3] W. Fitzgerald, *Africa*, Methuen.

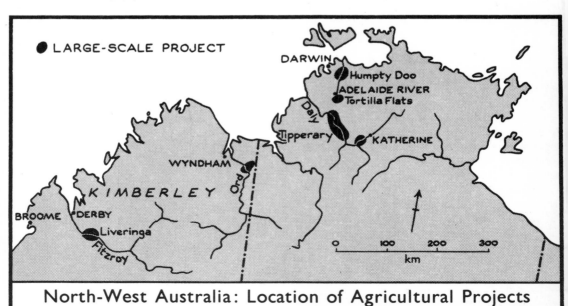

North-West Australia: Location of Agricultural Projects

pointer to the future lies in the pioneer settlement at present taking place in the Tunebia district of eastern Colombia.

This map shows the remote Tunebia region of eastern Colombia where in recent decades several attempts have been made to colonize the rain forest which lies beyond the Andean cordillera. The most successful effort[4] is taking place on the lower terraces of the rivers Cobaria and Cobugon, with San Luis del Chuscal as the main base camp. A Mission was established at San Luis in 1959 with the object of converting the local Tunebo Indians to Christianity and setting them up as farmers on cleared land in the adjacent valleys. A plantation system of farming is being introduced with coffee as the main cash crop, but cacao, bananas, plantains and maize are also grown. In spite of a lack of suitable pasture Zebu and crossed Zebu cattle have also been brought in and the region is now self-sufficient in milk. There are also pigs and poultry. In addition to the Tunebo converts the new settlers include refugees from western Colombia, families who cross the Andes to seek escape from civil strife and economic hardship. Of vital significance to the success of the settlements is the new Andean motor road—the Carretera del Sarare—which links Gibraltar to the main settled districts in the western part of the country. Coffee is exported along this route and via the older road through Guican to Pamplona.

4 For fuller details see D. R. Stoddart and J. D. Trubshaw, 'Colonization in Action in Eastern Colombia', *Geography*, No. 214, p. 47.

Rain-forest in Guyana. The Essiquibo River provides a highway through the dense network of trees. The houses in the clearing are for workers on a Colonial Development Corporation timber concession. Office buildings and dock and timber loading installations are also visible.

One major snag in any development scheme is the high cost of imported mineral fertilizers, without which outputs from Equatorial soils will inevitably decline. This problem can be eased by generating hydro-electric power and using it to produce nitrogenous salts: water power is readily available in all rain-forest regions. Many authorities deplore the lack of good tropical cattle: rain-forest regions desperately need a sturdy animal, resistant to heat, humidity and tsetse fly, in order to ensure a steady supply of animal protein and organic manure. It seems likely that modern scientific breeding techniques will produce such an animal in the foreseeable future: some new breeds such as the Santa Gertrudis (*see page* 43) already exist, but these

Pioneer Settlement in Eastern Colombia

are better adjusted to a savana rather than a rain-forest environment. The Report of the Forster Committee on possible agricultural developments in north-west Australia strongly recommends a combination of cash cropping and cattle fattening, with an emphasis on the latter.[1] Cattle and rice are specifically suggested for the hot, swampy 'Tortilla Flats' region, while at Katherine (*Map, p.* 34) 400 hectares of pastures sown in buffalo grass and Townsville lucerne carry up to 25 beasts per hectare, a notably high density in the hot, humid tropics. Another experimental station 13 kilometres south of Darwin (12° 20′ S. lat.) reports that 'given the right conditions, vegetables and fruit could be grown in commercial quantities'. Plants recommended as most suited to the rain-forest region of Australia are rice, pasture grasses, fodder crops, peanuts and cotton—in that order. It should be noted that the climate of north-west Australia has a distinctly 'Monsoonal' pattern, with a near-drought season lasting for four months in mid-winter.

rates to exhaust the soil moisture within root range and damage crops severely.[3]

Predictions are made difficult, too, by the lack of detailed climatic and soil information for enormous areas of rain-forest. Even where rainfall régimes are known, the exact effects of rainfall on soils and plants in deforested clearings can only be determined by actual cultivation. Soil variations also greatly affect the plants which can be grown: with tropical tree crops, for example,

> ... a tree species which requires $3x''$ of rain on clay soils will require $2x''$ on the sands.[4]

Details of this kind only become known as a result of research, but specialized tropical agricultural research institutions have only become established in recent decades, and huge gaps in knowledge remain to be filled. Considerable information about the agricultural potential of rain-forests

DARWIN (29·6 m) R.f.	°C	29	28	29	29	28	26	25	26	28	29	30	29	Total 1570
	mm	404	328	257	104	18	2	2	2	13	56	122	262	

Thus the suggested farming economy for north-west Australia would not necessarily suit rain-forest environments with a more evenly distributed rainfall. On the other hand many true rain-forests *do* have a less rainy season or even a brief dry period. This fact tends to be overlooked because of the evergreen vegetation, but

> ... many of the tree species of the evergreen forest have leathery, sclerophyllous leaves and other alleged adaptations to dry conditions.[2]

Where the total rainfall is approximately balanced by the total evaporation for the year '... even a relatively slight decline in the monthly receipt of rain, or pronounced irregularity in its distribution, may quite easily lead to serious shortages of water'. On deforested plots under cultivation a mere

> ... 14 days of drought, on lighter soils, may be more than enough at tropical evaporation

came from Belgian agronomists in the Congo, prior to the outbreak of political and military anarchy there in 1960. One group of experiments at Yangambi involved the cultivation of land on a 'corridor' system, in effect a sophisticated variant of shifting cultivation. A strip or 'corridor' of rain-forest was cleared each year, running from east to west so that it received the maximum amount of light from the short Equatorial days. Each corridor was about 30 metres wide and 1·6 kilometres long, and was planted with a rotation of crops for 3–6 years depending on local soil conditions. Prior to bring abandoned for a fallow period of 10–12 years the strip was planted with a tree crop such as banana to aid natural afforestation. Carefully organized clearing of this kind avoided some of the worst erosive effects of haphazard *ladang*. Attempts to develop trade by exporting food crops proved unprofitable because of transport difficulties.

[1] See R. G. Golledge, loc. cit.

[2] A. H. Bunting, 'Some Problems of Agricultural Climatology in Tropical Africa', *Geography*, No. 213.

[3] A. H. Bunting, loc. cit.

[4] Ibid.

Thus nearly a third of an acre of coffee shrubs per cultivator was henceforth incorporated in the scheme. The shrubs were planted in the mixed sandy and clay lands of the plateau, and to assist in the management of the crop they were grouped in a few large blocks. In 1953 the planting of some 2500 acres of oil-palm began somewhat nearer the river. Even more significant from the point of view of future trends was the fact that a grass sward had been established and that it was already supporting a number of beef cattle, which, it was hoped, would eventually be used as draught animals. The system was beginning to bear some resemblance to the intensive farming of Western Europe.[5]

The single largest region of sparsely settled rain-forest is Amazonia. This vast forested river basin extends over some 700 million hectares—two-fifths of the entire continent of South America—but contains only 3 million inhabitants. The inner lowlands, covering an area equal to that of France, Sweden, Poland, Germany, Spain and the British Isles combined, support only 2 million people, compared with the 250 million in these European countries. Population densities in Amazonia are scanty even by rain-forest standards: the Congo Basin, for example, is ten times more thickly peopled, though the physical environment is very similar. How does one explain the extraordinary emptiness of Amazonia? What possibilities are there of the region absorbing migrants from over-populated lands elsewhere?

The main reason for the lack of inhabitants lies in the disastrous history of Amazonia since Europeans first began to enter the region in considerable numbers in the 17th century. At that time there were many more groups of indigenous Indians, many of whom cultivated the alluvial soils bordering the major rivers. The rivers also provided them with fish and turtles and allowed them to develop some water-borne trade. This relatively civilized and prosperous economy was shattered by Portuguese merchant adventurers, who seized the riverine lands, massacred and enslaved the Indians and infected them with virulent diseases against which they had no natural immunity. The European intruders practised a pure 'robber economy', collecting such products as wild rubber, nuts, roots and fruit for export, but not investing the profits of their sales in the land. Labour was provided by surviving Indians, who soon lost the art of cultivation. Food for both white settlers and Indians has therefore to be brought in from outside. Even beans, one of the main staples of diet, must be shipped upstream from southern Brazil, in spite of the fact that they can be grown locally. Efforts to encourage cultivation have not met with much success.

Between Belém and Braganca, near the Atlantic coast, runs a railroad a hundred and eighty miles long. It was built partly for the purpose of encouraging agricultural development along its way in the hope that rural settlers would produce a surplus food supply for the city of Belém. Comparatively dense populations have grown up along the route of the railway, but subsistence gardening rather than commercial agriculture characterizes the husbandry of the people. Little surplus food is sent to Belém.[6]

The lack of cultivation is partly attributable to the landholding system, whereby the all-important river-banks are owned by a few large proprietors: in fact most peasants have no land and no prospect of access to the rivers.

... nearly all riparian lands throughout the inner basin are already in individual or corporate hands, either in fee simple or by government lease. When one considers the vast space of the valley, together with its sparse populations, it would appear without further examination that there is boundless terrain available for homestead settlement. But this is not the case, although the governments could, by changing their land lease policies, make it so. Even on the remote Casiquiare River ... every mile of stream bank is mapped, plotted and assigned to an owner or lessee. It is the same with all the thousands of miles of riparian lands, whether they are under the sovereignty of Brazil, Peru, Venezuela, Bolivia, Ecuador or Colombia. Not only is the fluvial basin definitely not *terra incognita* but its useful parts are already owned or assigned. ... in this region, one of the most sparsely populated in the world, 60 per cent of the rural people are already obliged to live and work on the estates of others because they have no land of their own. This is a fact deserving reflection by designers of resettlement schemes who dream of shifting land-hungry peasants from one

[5] Rene Dumont, *Types of Rural Economy*, Methuen, p. 43.

[6] Fairfield Osborn, *The Limits of the Earth*, Faber, p. 112.

continent to another—even the peon of the Amazon might apply.[1]

The landholding system is not an insuperable obstacle to progress, however, for it could be changed, and experiments show that commercial production of many food and tree crops is feasible in Amazonia. Cocoa, coffee and rubber plantations could be established on the sandy plateaus, and rice, maize, beans and water-melons would all do well on the alluvial floor-plains. The latter are in relatively short supply, but silt-trapping experiments in the middle and lower Amazon valley indicate that the areas of fertile alluvium could be greatly extended. If all these agricultural possibilities were realized Amazonia could absorb tens of millions of immigrants, but the situation is complicated by the fact that death-rates among the region's existing population are falling rapidly and total numbers are thus increasing. Some authorities predict an eventual effective occupation of Amazonia by 70–100 million indigenous inhabitants.

5. The Savana Lands

The Savanas are tropical grasslands extending over vast areas of Africa, northern Australia and Latin America. Broadly speaking they lie between Equatorial rain-forests on the one side and hot deserts on the other (*see map, p.* 10). Hence the natural vegetation of Savana lands, although basically grass with a few scattered trees, increases in luxuriance and includes an increasing proportion of trees towards the rain-forest fringe, but degenerates into thorn scrub on the margins of the deserts. These variations reflect differences in total mean annual rainfall and in the length of the rainy season, but all Savana lands experience a period of drought, so that irrigation is vital for effective crop cultivation. The climate figures for Bulawayo (21° S. lat.) indicate that there are in fact three seasons, viz. (i) relatively cool and dry ('winter'), (ii) hot and relatively dry and (iii) hot and wet ('summer'). Not only is Savana rainfall confined to one period of the year, it is notoriously variable, both in total and in duration. This applies especially to the drier Savanas,

1 Fairfield Osborne, op. cit.

e.g. northern Queensland, where the total annual rainfall can vary from 250 mm in one year to 1000 mm in the next. The failure of the rains can bring disaster to pastoralists and cultivators alike and is one of the prime reasons why huge areas of Savana are at present either little used or completely neglected. Yet many agronomists assert that of all the world's underdeveloped or undeveloped lands the tropical Savanas are potentially the most promising from the viewpoint of future agricultural productivity.

At present the major handicap of the Savanas is their inferior soils. These have been produced partly by the climate, but also in Africa and Latin America by generations of bad farming practices. Throughout the drought season soil moisture is constantly lost into the atmosphere by evaporation. This loss is in part made good by an upward movement (due to capillarity) of brackish ground-water. As the water evaporates, however, all dissolved salts are left behind at the ground surface. Long-continued accumulation of these deposits leads to the formation of a solid, infertile, saline encrustation several feet thick, called a *hard-pan*. Savana soils are also badly affected by *downward* leaching during the violent convection rainstorms of the hot, wet season. (For details of this type of soil depletion, *see pp.* 29–30.) Downpours are particularly heavy at the beginning of each rainy season, i.e. when the topsoil is parched and dry, and least able to withstand erosion. This seasonal alternation of sluicing and dessication leads to the formation of lateritic soils, composed almost entirely of iron and aluminium hydroxides, the valuable plant nutrients having been removed in solution.

Pure laterites are utterly infertile, but most Savanas support a covering of coarse, fibrous grasses. In addition there are clumps of trees, notably in damper hollows and along the banks of watercourses. In fact it is probable that large portions of the African Savana were formerly forested, the trees having been destroyed by generations of burning to make grazing grounds. Pastures produced in this way are maintained by setting fire to the grasses in the dry season to encourage the growth of young shoots. This leads to a progressive deterioration of both the soil and the grasses, the latter becoming less and less nourishing as time goes on. In spite of their low quality, however, Savana grasslands are at present used mainly for animal husbandry.

| BULAWAYO °C | 22 | 21 | 21 | 19 | 16 | 14 | 14 | 16 | 19 | 22 | 22 | 22 |
| (1363 m) R.f. mm | 140 | 122 | 114 | 20 | 15 | 0 | 0 | 0 | 8 | 15 | 79 | 120 |

Generally speaking, productivity is low, for the misused and scanty pastures can support relatively few animals, and these are markedly inferior to their counterparts in temperate lands. (*See page* 94). As well as suffering as a result of deficiencies in their feed, cattle on the Savanas are seriously affected by many parasites and diseases, some of the more damaging of which are mentioned in the notes overleaf.

Control of these various diseases is possible by means of vaccination, the slaughter of infected herds, and strict veterinary police measures. Among primitive nomadic herdsmen, however, such controls are difficult to implement. The owners do not understand the necessity for isolating or restricting the movement of their animals, and resent 'outside' interference. Furthermore the Savanas are so vast and remote, and the migratory habits of nomadic pastoralists so haphazard, that movement orders are impossible to enforce. The afflictions mentioned in the notes, p. 40, therefore continue to have a widespread impact, and animals on the Savana mostly belong to certain breeds of dwarf cattle, goats and sheep which are unusually resistant to disease.

Another factor making for low-grade animals is the traditional attitude with which most pastoral nomads regard their beasts. They are kept mainly for investment, ceremonial purposes and social prestige, the latter depending on the ownership of many animals, irrespective of their quality. Such an outlook leads inevitably to overstocking and overgrazing, with attendant destruction of both vegetation and soils. Constant close nibbling of young shoots leads to the disappearance of the better-quality grasses, and weeds soon take over. This in turn reduces the moisture content of the soil, which becomes dusty and wide open to wind erosion. The churning of the ground in the vicinity of overcrowded waterholes also leads to soil erosion by both wind and rain.

Pastoral nomads depend on their animals for food, but this is mainly in the form of milk and blood (tapped from veins), and beasts are rarely killed or sold for meat. There is therefore little or no concept of commercial stock-raising, or incentive to breed more productive animals. Commercial grazing *has* become well established, however, in the Savana grasslands of Australia and certain parts of Latin America. In both of

Native cattle on the savana, northern Ghana.

SOME MAJOR DISEASES WHICH ESPECIALLY AFFECT SAVANA ANIMALS

Trypanosomiasis ('sleeping sickness' in man) affects over 1000 million hectares of Africa south of the Sahara. The protozoa causing this disease are spread by tsetse flies as they move from beast to beast, sucking the animals' blood. Huge areas of the African Savana are virtually without horses, cattle and pigs, due to tsetse fly infestation. DDT spraying is very effective, the eggs being destroyed along shady watercourses. No successful livestock industry will be possible until eradication is complete. (*See also p. 93*)

Brucellosis, a bacterial disease causing undulant fever and abortion, is especially widespread among goats. It causes heavy loss of milk and kills large numbers of unborn kids and calves.

Tapeworms are intestinal parasites, causing serious debilitation, especially in cattle and pigs. The worms are easily passed on to humans beings via uncooked or partially cooked infected meat. In East Africa they are the most common intestinal parasite of rural natives. Autopsy reports there show that 90 per cent of persons examined are infected with beef-tapeworm.

Rinderpest (cattle plague) has in the past had catastrophic effects, especially throughout Africa. The disease is now controlled by vaccination.

Foot-and-mouth disease is the most contagious of all animal diseases. Although not necessarily fatal, it reduces the beef potential and the milk yields of cattle for the remainder of their lives.

Sheep-pox, a highly contagious disease similar to smallpox in man, can decimate whole flocks. It affects the nostrils, trachea, lungs and alimentary canal.

Newcastle disease affects poultry. Until recently it led to 70 per cent–100 per cent mortality in the Far East. It can now be controlled by vaccination, without which commercial poultry farming is very chancy.

A water-hole in the primitive and remote tribal area of the Karamoja, Uganda. Note the well trodden ground around the hole, a potential cause of soil erosion during the rainy season.

these continents the impetus has come from peoples of European descent, i.e. farmers with Western concepts of cash transactions and profit-making. To a much smaller extent similar developments have taken place in East Africa, notably in the former 'White Highlands' of Kenya.

Australia has important beef-cattle lands on the Savanas of the Queensland 'Downs', the Northern Territory and the Kimberley district of Western Australia. Cattle-runs here are the biggest in the world and for three generations cattlemen have raised animals in the 'Outback'. Unfortunately, the growth of the industry has been hampered by the following serious drawbacks:

1. The whole region (except the east coast plains of Queensland) suffers from occasional disastrous droughts.

2. Many of the best pasture lands are still hundreds of kilometres from the nearest railway.
3. Pastures are frequently damaged by pests such as rabbits, kangaroo and prickly pear, and cattle ticks infest the animals.
4. Labour is scarce, especially in the Northern Territory and Kimberley, because the hard, lonely pioneering life of an Australian cattleman attracts only real adventurers.

In the Northern Territory . . . were it not for the Australian aborigines the pastoral industry there would cease to function. Alexandria (a large cattle station) is actually clothing and feeding three tribes of 190 blacks to retain a constant strength of 60 stock-hands and house-'gins' . . . Some pastoral companies have seen the light, and are starting to provide improved living conditions for white men, including better housing and other amenities, to encourage station employees to marry and rear families.[1]

5. Lack of capital.

Today not more than six holdings in the Northern Territory have completely fenced boundaries. On some there is no fencing at all, except a horse-paddock. Almost as important as fencing is the provision of watering points. There is always a dry season . . . and if no rain falls during October and November thousands of cattle are lost through bogging in drying water-holes and others die when over-grazed land around water-holes is eaten out.[2]

[1] R. E. Cornish, 'Millions for Meat', *Geographical Magazine*.
[2] R. E. Cornish, loc. cit.

When cattle are ready for market they are sent to meat-packing works on the coast. For farmers within reach of a railway, this is easy; but the cattlemen of the remote inland pastures must first move their beasts to feeding grounds near a railhead. Until recently they were driven on foot for hundreds of kilometres along 'overlanding' routes, but now roads are being built and large motor trains carry the cattle in a fraction of the time formerly taken. Even so the animals lose weight en route and have to be fattened before slaughter. The photo below shows cattle jumping from a road train in Queensland.

Apart from the provision of water-holes, Savana livestock production in Australia remains largely unimproved and unscientific. A Government-sponsored research organization (C.S.I.R.O.) has in recent years investigated the possibility of improving pastures, for tropical Savana grasses wither in the dry season, becoming harsh and unpalatable, and cattle fed on them generally do not make first-class beef. Experiments with specially bred legumes and grasses show that it is possible, without irrigation, but using heavy concentrations of fertilizers, to increase grazing plants more than tenfold (from about 2000 to about 23 000 kg per hectare). The high cost of bringing fertilizers into such remote regions makes such methods only marginally economic, but the potential for increasing beef yields is clearly very great.

Latin America contains vast areas of largely unimproved Savana grasslands, mainly in the upper Orinoco Basin, and the *campos* of the

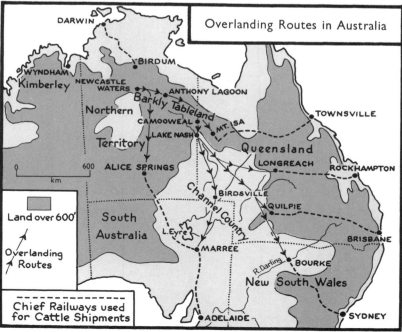

Overlanding Routes in Australia

(Above) *An artesian bore at Bedourie, western Queensland. Bores such as this give a reliable water supply to many cattle stations and townships in the remote outback. This bore, 4000 m deep, yields 6·38m, litres of water daily under natural pressure.*

(Below) *A water-hole in the Mitchell grass country of central Australia. Santa Gertrudis animals are converging on a 'turkey nest' dam on the Brunette Downs cattle station. Note the wind-pump which obtains water from a semi-artesian underground aquifer.*

Brazilian Plateau. On the *llanos* where Spanish settlers introduced Iberian cattle as early as the 16th century, conditions for pastoral farming are far from ideal, and well-run productive ranches are still in a tiny minority. This conspicuous lack of achievement is attributable to the natural hazards common to all Savana lands, but which affect the Orinoco Basin with unusual severity. During the long drought season (November to May) the grasses wither, fodder is in short supply, and cattle are forced to roam for months on a very inadequate diet. Then during the hot wet season (June to October) much of the Orinoco flood-plain is converted into an enormous, shallow-water swamp, relieved only by island-like interfluves where the cattle take refuge until the waters subside. For a brief period there is such an abundance of quick-growing fodder plants that the cattle over-feed and suffer from digestive ailments. In fact the grasses grow so quickly that they soon lose their palatability, and badly drained pastures on the lower land provide very inferior feed. Furthermore, a

general lack of flood control leads to the death by drowning of large numbers of cattle. The animals are mostly low-quality cross-breeds, the descendants of European cattle which have wandered semi-wild over the *llanos* for many generations.

In recent years a notable pioneer scheme designed to overcome these extremes of drought and flood has been put into effect by the Government in the Venezuelan State of Guárico.[1] This State contains 2·8 million hectares of Savana pastures and over 1 million cattle. A great rock and earth dam, 15·2 kilometres long, 183 metres wide and 30 metres high has been built across the Guárico River, to the north-west of Colabozo (*see map*). The dam holds back a lake, 233 square kilometres in area and containing more than 2000 million cubic metres of flood water. During the dry season this water is released to irrigate 110 000 hectares of land, via 480 kilometres of specially dug ditches and canals. The irrigated land has been carved into 550 ranches, each of 200 hectares. The carefully regulated supply of water is used to grow subsistence and fodder crops, and a sustained effort is being made to build up high-quality beef and dairy herds. All properties are fenced—in itself a revolutionary technique in the Savana—and are sown with specially bred varieties of drought-resistant grass. Trees are planted to provide shade so that the animals do not collapse from heat stroke during the hottest months. A research organization advises on all aspects of pastoral farming, individual farms being encouraged to seek help in such matters as soil surveys and the purchase of new varieties of grass. In addition a technical advice organization has been established to assist farmers with such matters as pest control, fertilizers and credit facilities. There are also communal facilities such as grass-drying plants, silos and warehouses. Further to offset the dangers of drought, hundreds of artesian wells have been drilled throughout the region, and natural depressions have been converted into permanent water-holes. Thousands of pedigree cattle have been imported to improve the meagre quality of the *llanos* herds. The pedigree beasts include Zebu, Santa Gertrudis (from Texas), Brahman, Swiss Brown and Holstein bulls. (*See photos*, page 87.)

1 See G. J. Butland, 'The Development of the Venezuelan Llanos', *Geography*, No. 196, p. 119. The account which follows is largely based on this article.

This enlightened scheme has now been operating for a decade and has proved so successful that it is hoped eventually to duplicate it in other parts of the Venezuelan *llanos*. Much depends, however, on the building of communications to the coast, for

the access of Guárico State to the major national markets of Valencia, Maracay and Carácas, all less than 200 miles distant and connected by good motor roads, was an important factor in the choice of this region for the scheme.[2]

Elsewhere in Latin America the Savana pastures remain comparatively remote from potential markets for beef and dairy produce.

6. The arid lands

Arid lands may be variously defined, but here the term applies to regions where farming would be impossible without irrigation. Both temperate and tropical arid lands have been farmed by means of irrigation since Neolithic times, but in recent decades increasingly sophisticated

2 G. J. Butland, loc. cit.

The Venezuelan Llanos & Guárico Dam

44

engineering techniques, especially in dam construction and pumping, have vastly extended the areas under cultivation. At the same time the two major problems of salination and/or waterlogging, which tend eventually to afflict irrigated farmland, have become highlighted to a dramatic degree. Consider, for example,

> The famed Al Kharj oasis in Saudi Arabia . . . Here in a two-thousand-acre tract is the model farm of King Ibn Saud. Under the direction of an American agricultural expert and staff and financed by the King's oil royalties, experiments are undertaken in the development of food and forage plants adapted to the Arabian environment. From the horticultural point of view the undertaking has been a distinct success, but in another respect it is probably doomed to eventual failure. The tract is watered from a deep natural reservoir, whose waters are hardly potable. Every irrigation channel is rimmed with alkaline salts. . . . From year to year as new sections are put to the plough others must be abandoned as no longer productive.[1]

The Nile Valley, Egypt. Irrigation canals permit cultivation, but where water is unavailable there is an abrupt transition to sand desert.

Salination on this scale arises when irrigation water is excessively saline, or when flushing of the encrusted salts is not feasible. Waterlogging also indicates unsatisfactory irrigation techniques, for swamp conditions arise when so much water is added to the land that the watertable is raised to ground level. However, it is not surprising that mistakes have been made, for the scientific study of deserts and their development is a product only of the last few decades. The desert environment is essentially hostile and settlers must contend with great extremes of heat and cold, dust, isolation and searing winds, as well as the overriding necessity of ensuring a supply of usable water. Possible sources of water include: 'exotic' rivers, i.e. rivers which rise outside but flow into or across an arid landscape; pumping water from below ground; the transfer of water into deserts from external rivers and lakes; sea-water distillation and deliberate changing of the climate (e.g. 'rain-making'). Each of these possibilities will now be considered.

Exotic rivers at present provide the bulk of water used for irrigation. The most famous are the Nile, Tigris, Euphrates, Ganges, Indus and Amu Darya; more recently important schemes have also been developed on the Snake, Colorado and Rio Grande in North America, and the Orange in South Africa. In addition there are hundreds of smaller streams and torrents which flow a few kilometres into the borderlands of deserts before they evaporate: irrigation water from such sources is obtained, for example, along the southern foothills of the Atlas Mountains in Algeria, the western foothills of the Andes in the Atacama and the northern edge of the Tien Shan in Soviet Central Asia.

In parts of the Middle East and Asia old-fashioned and relatively inefficient irrigation methods still persist. Annual floodwaters are trapped behind hastily constructed mud embankments, whilst in the slack-water season, water is pumped from the rivers by means of primitive lifting apparatus like the *shaduf* and *sakia* (*see photos*) to ditches and reservoirs on higher ground. On the Nile the area that can be irrigated in this fashion is limited to a strip about 460 metres wide on each river bank, and even with modern diesel pumps the width of the usable strip can only be increased to about 1½ kilometres.

[1] Dr. H. L. Hoskins, *Annals of The American Academy of Political and Social Science,* CCLXVIII, pp. 85–95.

(Above) *Nile Delta: irrigation by tambour (Archimedean screw)*.

(Left) *Nile Delta: irrigation by shaduf*.

Nile Delta: irrigation by sakia.

(Above) *Irrigation canals being constructed by hand labour, near Jaffna, Ceylon.*

(Below) *Irrigation canals being constructed by modern technology, Al Hassa Oasis, Saudi Arabia.*

This is due to the high cost of pumping water uphill, a cost which may exceed the value of crops from the newly irrigated farmland.

Modern irrigation schemes using river water involve the construction of large, costly dams. To make such schemes economic they are usually combined with other projects such as flood control, improvements in navigation, fisheries and hydro-electric power generation. Electricity produced on the spot is then used to pump water through a labyrinth of irrigation channels. Even so, the capital costs of dam-building may run into hundreds of millions of pounds. The new Aswan Dam on the Nile, for example, cost over £400 million loaned to the Egyptian Government by the Soviet Union. Costs on this scale obviously inhibit any rapid extension of irrigation in underdeveloped lands. Such costs are incurred both in the planning and construction of dams. Preliminary hydrological, geological and engineering surveys take years to complete. Thousands of workmen have to be recruited, housed, fed and provided with amenities for up to fifteen years at a remote desert location. Fleets of excavating and earth-moving vehicles must be hired, fuelled and maintained. Huge quantities of rock, sand and gravel must be quarried and assembled, together with imported cement and steel reinforcing rods. All tools, equipment and foodstuffs must be carried to the dam site from outside the desert often on specially built roads and railways. A system of pumps and irrigation channels must be laid out by constructional engineers. On rivers carrying a heavy load it may be necessary to construct anti-silt dams upstream from the dam, otherwise the reservoir will become choked with alluvium and rendered useless within a few decades. Still more expense is involved when, as in Egypt, an illiterate peasantry needs instruction in the efficient use of irrigation water, new crop rotations and fertilizers. The use of fertilizers is vital if the newly won land is to yield maximum crops. Fertilizers must also be applied on older irrigated land to replace silts which no longer reach downstream beyond the new dam during times of flood. Yet more costs are involved if attempts are made to reduce water losses from the reservoir by evaporation, losses which may remove up to 10 per cent of the total stored water. Experiments in Australia and elsewhere show that such evaporation can be cut by about one-third by smearing a reservoir with a very thin veneer of cetyl alcohol. At present, however, this substance is costly to produce in bulk, and it is only really effective on small water areas where wave action is negligible.

The greatest number of people dependent upon exotic river irrigation live in Monsoon Asia, where the problem is to conserve the torrential rainfall of the summer Monsoon so that it can be used throughout the remainder of the year. In the Indian sub-continent many canals, tanks and wells are of great antiquity, but under British rule a complex system of large dams and perennial canals was built in the Punjab and the Sind, so that irrigation came to account for nearly one-quarter of the total cultivated area. Since Partition in 1947 both India and Pakistan have undertaken many new schemes, the most remarkable being an extension of the works on the Indus. Here, in the Sind, the completion of the Sukkur or Lloyd Barrage has brought under cultivation an area almost equal to the entire cultivated land of Egypt. Before irrigation much of the great flood-plain of the Indus

> ... was a desolate place; the surface mostly bare, in places hard and smooth and almost impervious to water when rain fell, in places powdery with saltpetre, and in places growing some grass after rain. Belts of such open ground alternated with belts dotted with small hardy trees or shrubs, which tended to collect the moving sand and dust to form sandhills that in places formed a miniature Sahara ... Animal life is represented by snakes, lizards, and a few gazelles ... a few pastoral and nomad tribes lived a free but hard life, living precariously by their camels which could eat anything, and their cattle that seem able to exist on the smell of grass roots, finding sport and occupation in stealing cattle from each other and from riverain neighbours. The water-table was 80 to 120 feet below the surface; in the shallow valleys of a plain that is perfectly level to any but a trained eye, the collection of the annual rainfall of less than 6 inches gave better grazing, and here these Janglis ('jungle folk') had their regular camping places, at wells they had made ... holes, up to four feet in diameter and going into the bowels of the earth ... the huts were made of reed screens ...[1]

[1] O. K. H. Spate, *India and Pakistan*, Methuen, p. 467, quoting an unpublished paper by E. S. Lindley on 'The Canal System of the Punjab'.

During the past forty years this arid landscape has been transformed into one of the most prosperous agricultural areas in Asia, an area now threatened, however, by serious problems of salination and waterlogging.

The first dam on the Indus, the Sukkur Barrage, was completed in 1932: since then four more dams have been added, notably the Lower Sind Barrage (1955) and the Gudu Barrage (1962). The purpose of these dams is to raise the river level during the dry winter season so that water can continue to flow through a maze of irrigation canals throughout the year. Before the padi fields are ploughed they are carefully flooded to a depth of several centimetres and the water allowed to soak into the ground. At intervals of a few weeks a succession of similar floodings permits the growth of a great variety of both temperate and tropical crops (*see below*).

TYPICAL CROPS GROWN IN THE SIND IRRIGATION AREA (*See map overleaf*)	
cotton	carrots
rice	clover
millet	oilseeds
maize	sorghum

Difficulties arise for a variety of reasons. Above all there has been a disastrous rise in the water-table (level of saturation) transforming huge areas of formerly productive farmland into swamps

Modern dam building in West Pakistan.

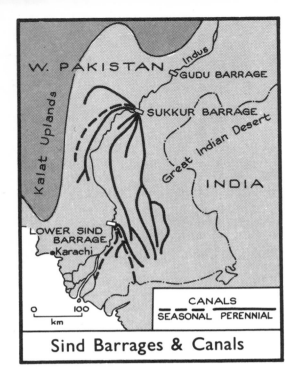

Sind Barrages & Canals

CANALS
SEASONAL — PERENNIAL

0 100
km

this procedure may well encourage the formation of swamps. A major difficulty inhibiting effective drainage is the extraordinary flatness of the Indus flood-plain, which during the last 1500 kilometres of the river's course falls a mere 200 metres. Another factor is the high permeability of much of the sandy alluvium, allowing some 40 per cent of water to soak away through the bottom of irrigation channels.

Deterioration of soils has now reached disaster proportions in West Pakistan, some 2·6 million hectares of land being affected by waterlogging and salination. This total is increased by between 20 000 to 40 000 hectares which go out of cultivation each year. In the upper Sind 27 per cent of the 1·5 million hectares under irrigation contains more than 0·4 per cent of salt and is therefore no longer economic to cultivate. Over 0·5 million hectares are similarly affected in the lower Sind and Indus Delta. In some localities, such as the Sheikhupura district of the Punjab, more than half of the cultivated area is either waterlogged or saline. An American team of consultant engineers which studied the problem on behalf of the Pakistan government recommend large-scale pumping as a means of reclaiming the ruined land. The salt encrustations can be dissolved away by pumping massive quantities of fresh water to the surface from underground. Much of the water will evaporate or be transpired into the air from the leaves of plants, but much will also sink back into the ground, carrying dissolved salts with it. The net loss of water by evaporation will lead to a gradual lowering of the water-table, so allowing the formerly flooded areas to be brought back into cultivation.

and/or saline mudflats. Salination accompanies a rising water-table due to the upward leaching of ground-water in conditions of rapid evaporation: as the water passes into the air the dissolved salts remain at the ground surface to form a continuously thickening salt crust. Salination also results from evaporation when irrigation water is allowed to spread too thinly over the fields: ideally enough water should be released during a controlled flooding to allow for *downward* leaching of excess salts. On the other hand

Fortunately the Indus ground-water is fresh enough for the vertical drainage scheme to succeed, and it is estimated that the total amount of water underground is equal to ten years' entire flow of the Indus. Power for the innumerable pumps needed can be obtained by using electricity from hydro-electric works connected with the irrigation dams, and Pakistan has also large reserves of natural gas which might be used.[1]

Waterlogging on very permeable soils can be prevented by abandoning surface flow in favour of spray irrigation. Spraying—in effect simulated

Salination of irrigated land in the Sind.

[1] Martin Simons, *Deserts: The Problem of Water in Arid Lands*, Oxford, p. 55.

rainfall—not only avoids the problem of drainage but also reduces the total water requirements for crop growth. Salination can be avoided by an occasional surface flooding to flush away the salts from amongst the roots.

Further development of spray irrigation may . . . open up areas that at the present time seem unpromising.[2]

As spraying is relatively expensive, this method of irrigation is only suitable with crops which command a high price.

The deposition of silt in the reservoir formed behind a dam can nullify the whole purpose of its construction. Reference has been made above to the construction of silt traps, but the effectiveness of such methods is limited. It is much more satisfactory to check erosion in the upper drainage basin, thus reducing the load of silt brought downstream. Erosion control entails keeping a strict supervision on farming methods, especially in the vulnerable headwaters region, and may well involve costly afforestation projects. Above all it means treating a river basin as a single entity, a difficult task if the basin happens to be shared between different countries, or even between different administrative units of a single state. The construction of the Aswan Dam, for example, became feasible only after prolonged

[2] *Guide Book to Research Data for Arid Zone Development,* ed. B. T. Dickson, UNESCO.

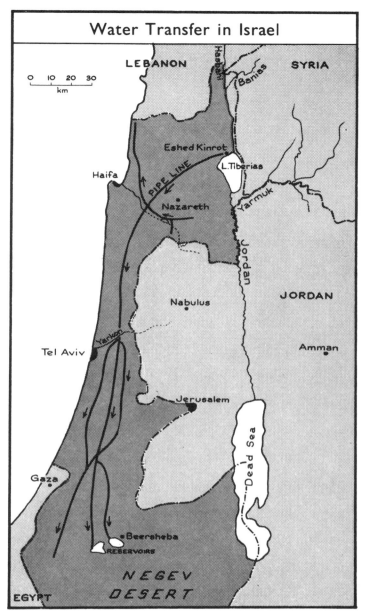

Water Transfer in Israel

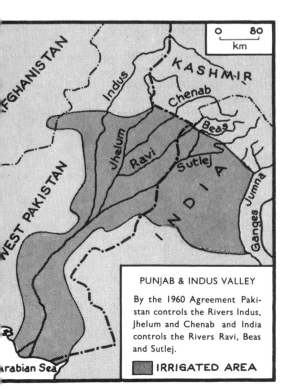

PUNJAB & INDUS VALLEY

By the 1960 Agreement Pakistan controls the Rivers Indus, Jhelum and Chenab and India controls the Rivers Ravi, Beas and Sutlej.

█ IRRIGATED AREA

This map (above) shows the Israeli–Arab frontiers prior to the 'Six Day War' of 1967. One bitterly contested dispute between Israel and her Arab neighbours concerns the use of the waters of the upper River Jordan. The map shows that Israel has built a system of pipe-lines to pump water from Lake Tiberias to the arid lands of the Negev. The Jordanians claim that this deprives them of the rightful water supply for irrigation projects in the lower Jordan Valley.

The map (left) shows the Punjab and Indus Valley, a cotton-growing region first developed under British rule by a remarkable network of irrigation canals. The waters which flow down from the Himalayan snows were used to transform the sun-baked desert of the Sind into fertile plains. In 1947, when the British Indian Empire was divided into India and Pakistan, the new frontier carved clean through the spider's web of channels.

Canals were cut off from their headstreams and irrigation ditches from their canals. After years of doubt in which cotton and wheat growers feared disaster, an agreement was reached in 1960 to share the waters of the 'land of the five rivers' as shown on the map. The area under scientific irrigation farming is to be greatly expanded, making possible a big increase in cotton production.

negotiations between Egypt and Sudan, and any attempt to reduce the silt load of the Nile would lead to political complications involving Ethiopia. The question also arises whether in fact dams should only be built in the upper part of a river basin. The danger of silting can then be minimized by submerging large portions of the steeper, vulnerable valley slopes. Water can then be distributed by gravity flow to all areas in the basin most suitable for cultivation. Details of notable disputes over the distribution of irrigation water are given on page 49.

Water pumped from below ground is already important in many arid regions, but recent discoveries of vast subterranean aquifers suggest that it should be possible greatly to extend the areas under cultivation, especially in the Near East and North Africa.

Of tremendous importance is the now verified existence of a vast freshwater reservoir which underlies a large part of the Sahara sand dunes. Recent research by the Service de l'Hydraulique of Algeria shows that the Albienne Nappe stretches for over 800 kilometres south from the Atlas ranges and it may also extend under Tunisia and the deserts of the Fezzan in Libya. The layer of water, which is estimated to be up to 1000 metres thick, absorbs at least 1000 million cubic metres of water per year from the Atlas rains. Another large underground reservoir stretches north from the Ennedi hills in (former) French Equatorial Africa towards Egypt, reaching the Qattara depression near El Alamein. Utilization of these waters, which are replenished from the heavy rainfalls enjoyed by mountainous regions to the north-west and south of the Sahara, may ultimately transform a part of what has always been regarded as the desert par excellence of the world.[1]

[1] *Possibilities of Increasing World Food Production*, F.A.O., p. 69.

Certain problems arise in the use of ground water. For example, great care must be taken in siting a major well. The diagram shows that if it is placed too close to existing wells, or if a great volume of water is extracted, the water-table will fall below the bottom of all shallower wells in the region and put them out of action. Furthermore it is advisable not to pump water out from an aquifer faster than it is being recharged: such action will not only lead to diminishing supplies but might well cause increasing contamination by salt. This has happened, for example, in the Santa Clara Valley to the south of San Francisco where excessive pumping has so depleted the aquifers that sea-water has seeped far inland. Similar problems affect ground-water irrigation schemes adjacent to the Aral and Caspian Seas in the Soviet Union. Even so, the whole of West Turkmenistan, an industrial region with oil wells, towns and ports, relies entirely on subterranean water drawn from below an almost waterless desert. Contamination of ground-water by sea water seepage has also occured in Australia, where many arid districts depend for their development, on artesian water supplies. The principal Australian aquifers are indicated on the map. Some of the deeper Australian wells reach down below 1200 metres. In fact the quality of the water in many Australian wells improves with depth, an unusual feature, for in most aquifers elsewhere the fresh water forms a high-level 'cream' floating on denser, saline water. As most ground-water is saline to a greater or lesser degree, research stations in many countries produce water-softeners and de-mineralizers so that the saltier water can be used. Desert dwellers also seek to improve the salt tolerance of both plants and animals by selective breeding. In Transcaucasia, for example, there are now karakul sheep which can thrive on the very high salt content of 16 grammes of salt per litre in their drinking water.[2]

[2] See Vladimir N. Kunin, *UNESCO Courier*, July–August, 1964, p. 17.

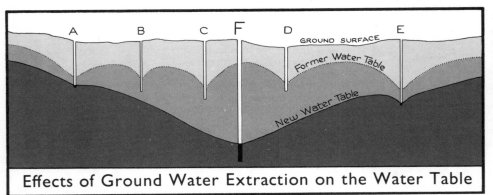

This diagram shows the effect on older, relatively shallow wells, of constructing a large modern pumping station. The large scale extraction of ground water from the new well **F** causes the water table (level of saturation) to drop to such an extent that the older wells **B**, **C** and **D** become completely dry, whilst those at **A** and **E** have much reduced water-holding capacities.

Effects of Ground Water Extraction on the Water Table

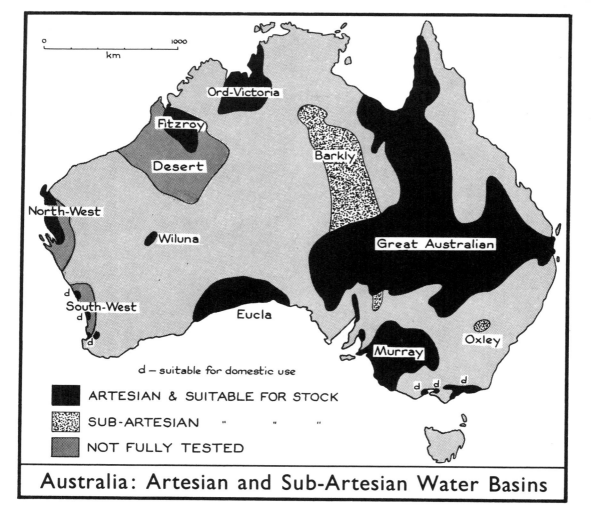

Ord-Victoria

Fitzroy

Desert

Barkly

North-West

Wiluna

Great Australian

d
South-West
d
d

Eucla

Oxley

Murray

d   d   d

d — suitable for domestic use

ARTESIAN & SUITABLE FOR STOCK

SUB-ARTESIAN " " "

NOT FULLY TESTED

Australia: Artesian and Sub-Artesian Water Basins

Most arid regions contain dry stream beds or wadis marking the course of rivers which flow only during infrequent rainstorms. Underground water is almost always present within the permeable sand and gravel on the beds of such streams. This water can be pumped up and used for cultivation, but flash-floods make wadis notoriously dangerous locations for settlement. Of more potential value for farming are the floors of inland drainage basins, such as the *sebkhas* of the Sahara. Drought-resistant swamp vegetation encourages solonchaks (desert soils) to develop on the floors of these salt-pans. During periods of drought, solonchaks tend to break up and become dusty, and so an accumulation of fertile silt is frequently dumped by the wind on the lee side of a pan. Such mounds of silt, called *lunettes* in Australia are not contaminated by salt because they are leached during rainfall. Thus

they provide useful patches of soil for desert cultivation.

The transfer of river water into deserts has already proved successful in several arid regions. In the Soviet Union, for example, the Kara-Kum Canal (*map, p. 52*) leads water from the Amu Darya, at Kerki, westwards to the oases of Mary, Tedzhen and Ashkhabad. This irrigation scheme is at present being extended to bring life-giving water to an immense area of barren desert in southern Turkmenistan. A major task is to prevent silt from the Amu Darya entering and choking the Canal. Some silt is removed by pumping, the rest by allowing it to settle on the beds of the Kelif Lakes through which the river water passes before entering the Canal proper. Problems also arise from water weeds which, unless they are removed by special cutting machines, clog the Canal and restrict its flow.

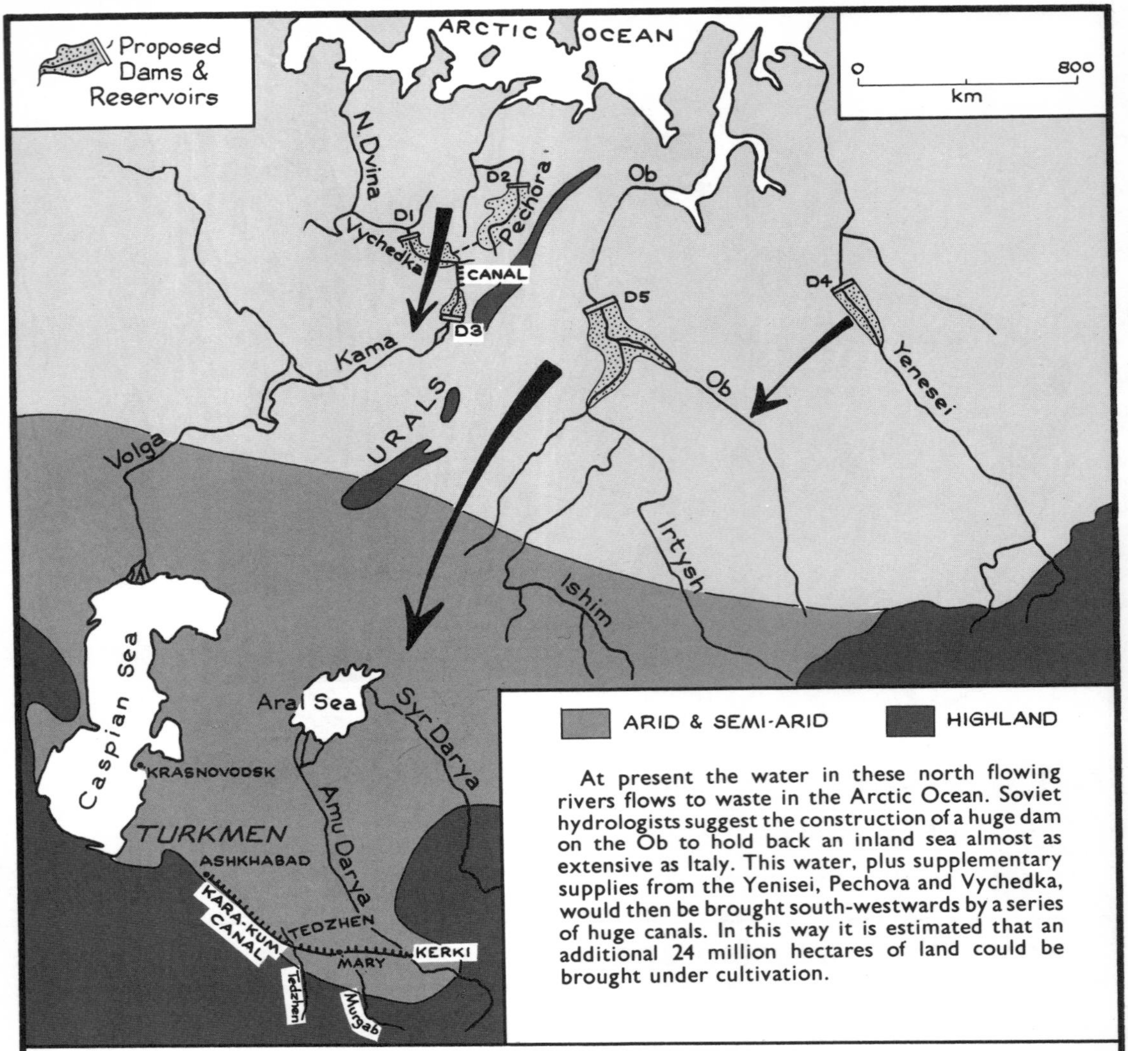
Proposed Dams & Reservoirs
ARCTIC OCEAN
0 800 km
N. Dvina
D1
D2
Pechora
Vychedka
CANAL
D3
Ob
D4
D5
Kama
Yenesei
URALS
Ob
Volga
Irtysh
Ishim
Caspian Sea
Aral Sea
Syr Darya
KRASNOVODSK
Amu Darya
TURKMEN
ASHKHABAD
KARA-KUM CANAL
TEDZHEN
MARY
KERKI
Tedzhen
Murgab
ARID & SEMI-ARID
HIGHLAND
At present the water in these north flowing rivers flows to waste in the Arctic Ocean. Soviet hydrologists suggest the construction of a huge dam on the Ob to hold back an inland sea almost as extensive as Italy. This water, plus supplementary supplies from the Yenisei, Pechova and Vychedka, would then be brought south-westwards by a series of huge canals. In this way it is estimated that an additional 24 million hectares of land could be brought under cultivation.
Proposed Diversion of Soviet Rivers which drain to the Arctic Ocean

Additional water enters the Canal from reservoirs on the Rivers Murgab and Tedzhen. The large new Khauz Khan Reservoir, due for completion in 1970, will enable the entire flow of the River Tedzhen to be diverted for irrigation. It is planned eventually to extend the Canal to Krasnovodsk on the Caspian Sea.[1]

A scheme has been envisaged to transfer vast quantities of water from the Rivers Ob and Yenisei to irrigate the arid steppe of Kazakhstan and the Turgay Lowlands (*see map*).

Large-scale water transfer schemes also operate in the U.S.A. In California, for example, the Rivers Sacramento and San Joaquin do not supply enough water to irrigate all the cultivable land of the arid Great Valley. The main shortage of water is felt towards the southern end of the Valley and to remedy this deficiency several aqueducts have been built to bring in water from outside rivers. The locations of these waterways are shown on the map, together with details of the water movements involved. An even larger scheme has been proposed to take water over and through the Tehachapi Mountains to Los Angeles and the Mohave Desert. This would complete a programme of work known as the Central Valley Project. At present the Project, backed by the U.S. Bureau of Reclamation, aims

[1] See Paul E. Lydolph, *Geography of the U.S.S.R.*, John Wiley p. 194.

to double the amount of irrigated land in the region. To this end 48 dams, 20 large canals, hydro-electric power plants and other works are being constructed. When completed the Project will provide water for over 1·2 million hectares of irrigated land, and double the number of farms in the Central Valley. In addition it should foster the growth of industry by providing adequate water and power, as well as giving complete control over flooding and salinity. The man-made lakes are to be developed as a tourist attraction. Doubts have arisen as to whether enough capital can be raised to enable the Project to be completed in its entirety. This is worth noting, for if financial problems afflict water transfer schemes in such a wealthy country as the U.S.A. the possibility of implementing similar projects in underdeveloped arid lands is not very strong. This should be borne in mind when considering the economic feasibility of such grandiose proposals as diverting some or all of the waters of the Rivers Niger and Congo into the Sahara, or the upper headwaters of the River Amazon into the Atacama.

Desalination of sea-water, cheaply and in vast quantities, has always been a tantalizing dream of people in arid lands. Now, with research teams in several countries striving for ever-cheaper desalination plants, it seems probable that this dream will be realized. Numerous

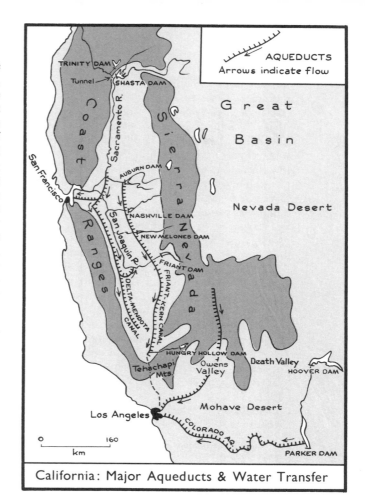

California: Major Aqueducts & Water Transfer

The Delta-Mendota Canal, part of the California Central Valley Project.

desalination plants already function, but at present they are only economic in special geographical situations. In Kuwait, for example, a series of large-scale water distilleries yield more than 45 million litres of water a day. These distilleries, powered by locally produced oil and natural gas, have been built during the past two decades in association with the development of Kuwait's vast petroleum resources. Formerly all the water used in Kuwait was imported. A similar situation exists on the completely waterless island of Aruba, off the coast of Venezuela. A large distilling plant there has been combined with an oil- and gas-fired power station. This plant supplies about 16 million litres a day for use in the refinery and an equal amount for the 54 000 inhabitants of the island. In both Kuwait and Aruba, however, immense capital resources are available from the wealthy oil industry.

For general purposes, including irrigation, a way must be found to bring down the cost of desalting. In the U.S.A. a government agency called the Office of Saline Water was set up in 1952. This Office has built five experimental plants, each of which uses a different desalting technique.[1] The plants at Freeport (Texas),

[1] Desalting techniques include multi- and flash-distillation, electrodialysis, freezing and the 'squeezing' of salt molecules through plastic pores.

Webster (South Dakota) and San Diego each have a production capacity of 4·5 million litres a day. Since 1952 the costs of desalting in the U.S.A. have fallen from $1.10 per 1000 litres to $0.22, as compared with an average cost of $0.09 for municipal water delivered to the public. In 1967 a government-supported water desalination research centre was established in Britain at Troon in Ayrshire. The centre's engineers hope to build a combined nuclear power station and distillation plant which would have a capacity of 400 megawatts and could produce 270 million litres of fresh water a day. The water would cost about 5s. a thousand litres, i.e. about twice as much as the average paid by water authorities in Britain. Research at Troon will concentrate on lowering this cost to make it compete economically with conventional storage and distribution methods. Meanwhile a Swiss engineering corporation claims that a plant it is constructing in Tunisia will produce between 500 000 and 2 250 000 litres of water a day at a cost twenty times cheaper than that of all existing methods.

Changing the climate of certain arid regions is probably feasible, but as yet no large-scale attempts have been made to test the various hypotheses which have been put forward. All deserts include large deflation depressions and

Desalination plant at Eilat, Israel. Photo. taken looking East across the Gulf of Akaba.

inland drainage basins. Examples include the Qattara in Egypt, the El Djouf and Bodélé basins in the Sahara, the Lake Eyre basin in Australia, the Caspian and Aral Sea basins in the Soviet Union and the Shotts of Tunisia and Algeria. If these basins were pumped full of sea-water—several of them which lie below sea-level would fill by gravity flow—the creation of large inland seas would, it is claimed, induce a wetter climate in the surrounding regions. Evidence to support this claim comes from the Soviet Union, where very large lakes have been created by damming rivers such as the Volga and the Dnieper. Small but appreciable increases in rainfall have also been reported from newly irrigated areas in Australia, the U.S.A. and the Middle East. The creation of a saline sea within a desert would, however, involve a salt accumulation problem, due to intensive evaporation.

On a smaller scale notable success has been achieved with rain-making techniques. The two main methods employed are (i) the 'seeding' of clouds and (ii) the creation of local convectional turbulence by intensive heating of the air. The first technique utilizes the fact that even in a desert clouds do at times develop at high altitudes, but rain rarely falls from them because the water droplets are so minute that they are kept aloft by strong convectional updraughts. By spraying the clouds with frozen carbon dioxide crystals or silver iodide, the condensed water particles multiply in number and merge together to form larger heavier raindrops. The rate of condensation increases because the spray supplies microscopic 'dust' nuclei or 'seeds' around which the invisible water vapour can condense: in non-desert air such nuclei are present naturally and include salt grains derived from the sea, and minute ice crystals. Clouds can be 'seeded' either directly from an aircraft, or by firing rockets or explosive shells from the ground, or (less satisfactorily) simply by burning coke impregnated with silver iodide in a line of braziers placed upwind from the target.

Since 1957 a series of Government-sponsored experiments in cloud seeding has been conducted in southeast Australia. Pairs of regions (*map, p.* 57) on the western slopes of the Great Dividing Range have been seeded simultaneously and then separately for periods of 10 to 12 days. Silver iodide smoke, generated by burning an acetone solution in a pressure type burner under an aircraft's wings, is sprayed into the base of clouds where the temperature is between $-5°C$ to $-10°C$. Approximately 1 kg of silver iodide is released every hour, i.e. about 10^{14} nuclei of iodide for every kilometre travelled by the aircraft. Results are distinctly encouraging. Rain usually falls about 20 minutes after spraying and continues to fall for about 60 to 80 minutes. The heaviest rain is obtained from cumulus clouds whose tops are colder than $-10°C$. The yield of water is enormous, one million tonnes of water being obtained for the expenditure of a mere 10 to 20 grammes of silver iodide.

In both the New England and the Snowy Mountains regions an increase in rainfall of approximately 30 per cent has been recorded in the first year of spraying, and there is a remarkable (and as yet unexplained) cumulative effect which lasts for several years. These experiments indicate that relatively large areas of eastern Australia are suitable for cloud seeding, in fact various State Agricultural Departments, River Authorities and Forestry Commissions now utilize cloud seeding as a regular means of increasing rainfall. In Victoria, for example, the Forests Commission sprays silver iodide over the tinder-dry Gippsland forests during the critical drought months of January, February and March, to maintain the forests in a damp condition and prevent a flare-up. The New South Wales and Victorian Departments of Agriculture have also been used cloud seeding over their wheatlands, including the semi-arid regions of Mallee and Wimmera, with very pleasing results. Following seeding in 1966, for example, the New South Wales wheat crop reached near record proportions.

The procedures for seeding over large areas are now well established and the costs can be quite accurately assessed. Over average terrain in a continental interior the cost is approximately £25 000 per annum per aircraft. This figure includes all operational costs, the salaries of air crew, seeding materials and other running costs but does not cover scientific management or the cost of collecting and analysing data. If special navigational or weather hazards exist in the region, more sophisticated equipment would be required and the cost might then increase by a factor of two or three. A single aircraft and crew can effectively seed an area of 25 000 square

kilometres, which leads to an overall cost of less than one penny per acre per annum.

This has to be matched against the potential financial return from any additional rain which falls. This, of course, is a highly variable figure depending on the field of application. In a hydro-electric catchment area, of which the operation in Tasmania is a typical example, an immediate cash return is obtained for addition water in the dams without further capital expenditure for generating machinery. Under these conditions it has been reliably estimated that a one per cent increase in precipitation pays for the whole operation; a 10 per cent increase represents a handsome profit.

In purely agricultural regions the break-even point is more difficult to assess and in some circumstances an increase of as much as five per cent in precipitation may be required to pay off. However, in other cases timing is of critical importance and some of these may be even more profitable than the hydro-electric case quoted above. For example, in the Mallee-Wimmera region of Victoria the wheat yield is critically dependent on the amount of rain falling during the growing season which extends from August 1st to October 31st. It has been conservatively estimated that an additional 2·5 cm of rain during this period represents a gain of £1 million in the wheat yield of the region. The cost of seeding the area for the three months period would not exceed £6000, giving a break-even figure of one half of one per cent. This was the situation which the Victorian Department of Agriculture exploited during 1966.

These figures bring out the fact that there is a huge discrepancy between the rainfall increase which can be detected by the usual methods of statistical assessment and that which is needed to confer a reasonable economic gain. Many of the conventional types of cloud seeding experiment may be required to continue for five or

These remarkable photographs were taken in S. E. Australia during 'rain-making' experiments over the Great Dividing Range. They show the effects of 'seeding' the base of clouds with silver iodide smoke. The sequence of events from initial seeding (top) to the formation of towering cumulonimbus (bottom) covers a period of 18 minutes. Heavy rain fell from the base of the 'seeded' clouds, after which a gap formed in that part of the cloud cover.

ten years before an increase of 10 or 20 per cent can be detected by the usual tests. At the same time an increase of a mere one per cent in the rainfall in the same region might represent a handsome pay-off in economic terms. There is a pressing need either for more sensitive tests than those at present in use or for a realistic test on the cost-effectiveness of the operation.[1]

Experiments in several countries show that an intense fire can cause a local convectional rain-storm, even in an arid region. This has also been observed to happen with bush fires in Australia and California, and with blazing oil-wells in North Africa.

In France experiments have been performed with a *meteotron*, which is a hexagonal arrangement of oil burners extending over an area of about four thousand square yards. The burners use a tonne of fuel oil each minute, but if they

[1] Cloud Seeding, E. G. Bowen, *Science Journal*, August 1967.

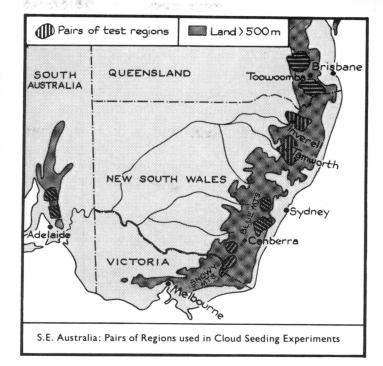

S.E. Australia: Pairs of Regions used in Cloud Seeding Experiments

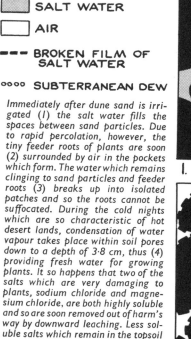

- ⊚ ROOT HAIRS
- ■ SAND PARTICLE
- ▨ SALT WATER
- ☐ AIR
- --- BROKEN FILM OF SALT WATER
- ∘∘∘∘ SUBTERRANEAN DEW

Immediately after dune sand is irrigated (1) the salt water fills the spaces between sand particles. Due to rapid percolation, however, the tiny feeder roots of plants are soon (2) surrounded by air in the pockets which form. The water which remains clinging to sand particles and feeder roots (3) breaks up into isolated patches and so the roots cannot be suffocated. During the cold nights which are so characteristic of hot desert lands, condensation of water vapour takes place within soil pores down to a depth of 3·8 cm, thus (4) providing fresh water for growing plants. It so happens that two of the salts which are very damaging to plants, sodium chloride and magnesium chloride, are both highly soluble and so are soon removed out of harm's way by downward leaching. Less soluble salts which remain in the topsoil are flushed out during the next irrigation.

Diagram to show plants growing in sand can avoid excessive salination even if irrigated with strongly saline water. (After Boyko.)

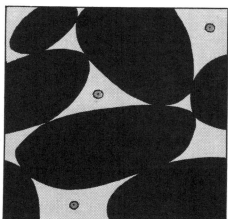

1. Salt water irrigation

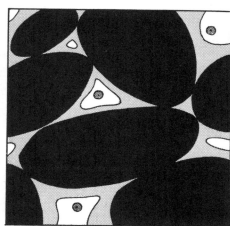

2. Partial root contact

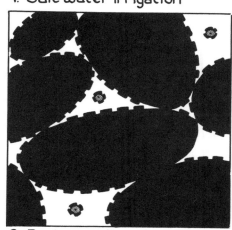

3. Broken salt water film

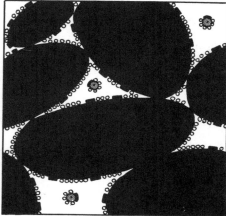

4. Subterranean dew

are lit at the right moment it is claimed that they can produce a growing rain cloud within six minutes. Small tornadoes have been created by this device, and on a number of occasions rain has actually fallen.[1]

The application of 'seeding' and firing techniques of rain-making to irrigation farming is at present inhibited by (*a*) their relatively high costs and (*b*) their unpredictability—it cannot be guaranteed that rain will fall on a particular patch of land. The Australian experiments, however, indicate that cloud seeding is an ideal

[1] Martin Simons, op. cit., p. 72.

way of obtaining a supply of additional water more or less uniformly over millions of hectares of arable land like the wheat regions of Victoria and New South Wales. In such vast regions it is not essential to obtain absolute precision in the rain 'target area'.

Traditional methods of desert reclamation have been based on the assumption that salt water is useless for cultivation. This view has been challenged in a remarkable series of experiments carried out in Israel since 1949 by Dr. Hugo Boyko. Dr. Boyko set out to prove that desert irrigation with saline water is possible provided that plants are grown in unconsolidated dune sand or gravel. Such highly permeable deposits, unlike soils which contain particles of clay, do not facilitate the build-up of salt residues which prove fatal to plants. The diagram on p. 57 gives full details.

At Eilat, in the blistering aridity of an almost absolute desert environment (mean annual rainfall less than 25 mm), Dr. Boyko began his experiments by planting 200 species of plants of which only a handful were known to be salt-resistant. Planting took place in a 'garden' covering 2·4 hectares, and the only water supply came by pipeline from two saline springs and later from the eastern Mediterranean. The soil in the garden consisted of 96·3 per cent stones and sand, 2·7 per cent silt and 1·0 per cent clay. The salinity of the irrigation water was deliberately varied between 2‰ and 35‰, so that controlled experiments could be conducted with waters having salinities equivalent to those of the local Negev springs (2‰–10‰), the North Sea (20‰–27‰), the Caspian and Aral Seas (10‰–13·25‰) and average oceanic water (35‰). A corresponding series of experiments were also made with fresh water.

Our results with the fodder plant *Agropyrum junceum* deserve special attention in the search for potential future food plants. This species has already been crossed successfully several times with wheat. We achieved seed production in our experiments at oceanic salt concentration and it is now only a matter of crossing suitable varieties of *Agropyrum* and wheat before we obtain one or more wheat varieties which can be directly irrigated on sand with

This 'desert garden' at Eilat was planted in 1949 on bare hills of sandy gravel (top) and irrigated with highly saline spring water. The bottom photo shows the same slope ten years later, luxuriant with Tamarix, Washington filifera, Juncus maritimus, Clerodendrum fragrans and Yucca aloifoali.

sea-water from the ocean. So far, the highest concentration for growing wheat was used successfully by a team of scientists at Bhavnagar in India. Their irrigation water was taken from the Indian Ocean and diluted to 20‰, which is still an extremely high concentration.

The important general conclusions from our experiments after two or three years of irrigation with salt water were as follows. Even the least salt-tolerant species could be grown successfully on dune sand irrigated with sea-water with a minimum chloride content about 20 times that hitherto considered permissible; other economically valuable plants could be raised using water with a salt content even 50–100 times higher. Chemical analyses made throughout the experiments proved that, contrary to the opinion prevailing among many soil and irrigation experts, no salt accumulation took place in the root layer of the soil, nor is any to be feared. Indeed after all these years of continuous irrigation with concentrations previously unheard of, the salt content of the soil was lower than before the experiments were launched. This is particularly significant for all arid zones.[2]

In the garden at Eilat almost all of the original plants survived and most of them flourished. Common vegetables and fruits which did well include melons (both water and sugar varieties), spinach, tomatoes and eggplant. A small eucalyptus sapling planted on the wet foreshore of the Red Sea (salinity 40‰) is now 12 metres high. The Negev saline-water cultivation experiments have recently been followed up in various hot desert environments, and successes have been reported with barley, artichokes, lucerne, carrots and asparagus in Tunisia, trees and shrubs in Kuwait, and wheat and plants yielding edible oils in India (at the Central Salt and Marine Chemicals Research Institute, Bhavnagar). Similar experiments in temperate lands have also been encouraging: for example food and fodder crops have been grown in sand on the marine foreshore at Oriñon in Spain, and pastures in Sweden have been successfully irrigated with water from the Baltic Sea (salinity 6‰–8‰). In the light of these successes it seems likely that farming with salt water will become increasingly important.

Grain size, calcium content and various other factors can influence the amounts of fertilizers needed and the time that can be allowed to elapse between each irrigation. . . . In general, however, the basic principles of salt-water agriculture hold true for all regions.

The first large-scale commercial enterprise using salt water for irrigation on sand has now been set up by the Desert Development Corporation, New York, on a desolate sand desert in the southern Negev in Israel. There, on an area of 800 hectares, a plantation of Juncus-Esparto (a perennial variety of *Juncus maritimus* with particularly good qualities for high-class paper pulp) has been started after extensive field experiments and technological tests and is now almost ready for its second harvest. The irrigation water is pumped from a large underground sea of saline water with a salinity of about 4% to 6% of which 2% to 3% is sodium chloride. Sand deserts with similar, and in most cases much better, conditions cover vast areas in all the continents. Our present experience indicates that a great variety of vegetables, cereals and fodder plants can easily be grown on these deserts. If financial and technological aid can also be found for those sand deserts to which brackish water or sea water has to be transported from greater distances, then completely new vistas are opened up for food production on a world scale. Atomic energy will probably be used for gigantic projects of this kind in the course of the next 10–20 years. Even now, for instance, serious negotiations are under way for bringing water from Canada to the arid parts of the United States and to Mexico. It is certainly not a Utopian idea to use brackish water or sea water, pure or partly desalinated, for farming the deserts. It is only a matter of carrying out more and larger experiments with more and still better varieties of plants under the most diverse conditions possible. These experiments will have to be carried out in the same way as experiments in traditional agriculture, using all the food and fodder plants known.[3]

Another unconventional approach to desert reclamation is being developed by the petrochemical industry. Esso scientists, for example, have developed a petroleum mulch which when sprayed over sand prevents the grains from drifting and also seals in moisture.[4] Experiments over

[2] Hugo Boyko, 'Farming the Desert', Science Journal, May, 1968.

[3] Hugo Boyko, loc. cit.
[4] See, Esso Magazine, Summer, 1967.

several thousand hectares of sand dunes in North Africa have resulted in the growth of tall luxuriant trees where formerly no tree could survive. In Arizona, petroleum mulches have been sprayed over ground used for growing cotton. The dark colour of the mulch absorbed and 'trapped' more of the sun's heat than did the untreated soil, and led to an increase in cotton yields by 33 per cent. Spectacular results have also been achieved with edible crops such as carrots, lettuce, radishes, melons, turnips and onions. Similar successes with vegetables have been reported from Libya, the Lebanon and Tunisia.

Animal husbandry has for centuries been the most important form of land use in the semi-arid zones of the Old World, and, despite the impressive developments in irrigation just quoted commercial grazing offers the best short-term means of improving the productivity of most semi-deserts in both hemispheres. This applies particularly to those regions where generations of farmers have so mis-used the land that they have made it even more arid. In southern Southwest Africa, for example, very large areas have become more desiccated as a result of two centuries of burning, overgrazing and tree-felling. A similar pattern of mismanagement has produced the so-called 'desert' of Rajasthan. This arid region is steadily encroaching eastwards and absorbing cultivated land on the Ganges flood-plain. It is thought that Rajasthan

was formerly covered with grasses, bushes and scattered trees, but has been transformed by centuries of overgrazing, burning and the cutting of trees and bushes for fuel or to provide emergency feed for livestock.[1] The Government of India has instituted a large-scale project to manage the livestock industry in the 'desert', with the regeneration of vegetation cover as a main priority. In conjunction with this reclamation scheme the Government of Uttar Pradesh has planted a protective shelter belt of forest to stabilize the sand and stop the eastward spread of the 'desert'. (*See map*).

Generally speaking desert ranges can best be improved by modifying the traditional methods of livestock farming so that no damage accrues to the vegetation cover. For example in many arid lands cattle are allowed to concentrate around water-holes: this leads to soil compaction, reduced permeability, more rapid run-off and in time to gully erosion. The more scientific systems of 'New World' commercial pastoralists keep the animals scattered, so ensuring more uniform grazing and reducing the danger of producing bare patches completely devoid of vegetation. A country with much experience of semi-arid livestock farming is Australia, where wide areas of grazing land do not receive more than 250 mm of rainfall a year. It has been found that cattle withstand such arid conditions better than sheep. Interior Australia is still a land of pioneer settlement, and as the better-watered areas become fully settled and developed, land-hungry farmers will inevitably be forced into the so-called 'desert' country. Hitherto the carrying capacity of the 'outback' has remained rather low, averaging 1–4 animals per square kilometre, but it is thought that improved techniques would make this type of farming more productive. A long list of recommended improvements includes: mechanization; more animal and plant breeding; fencing; an increase in the use of green fodder; a more efficient transportation and marketing system; the re-seeding and regeneration of pastures; the creation of fodder reserves for emergency drought years and the provision of carefully supervised 'fattening areas' in irrigated oases so as to relieve browsing pressures from the natural grazing lands. Clearly, such improvements are costly, and investments may not show a dividend for ten to fifteen years. Hence

[1] See B. T. Dickson (ed., op. cit., p. 159.)

Location of Rajasthan 'Desert' & Shelter Belt

individual farmers, always fearful of losing everything in a disastrous drought, tend to neglect their land (*see also p.* 41).

These recommendations apply with equal force to arid regions in the Old World, to lands such as Arabia, Iraq and North Africa which have old-established traditions of nomadic pastoralism. In these cases, however, a balance has to be struck between modernization for commercial gain and the possible destruction of proud, colourful, independent tribal groups. One example of the way in which traditional practices can be inter-woven with modern techniques was demonstrated by the French in Algeria, who established 'Improvement Centres' for nomadic herdsmen. These Centres provided an insurance scheme against drought, linked with large-scale reserve fodder dumps.

Reserves may be standing crops of grass, protected during the growing season, for use in a critical period of fodder shortage, or crops specially grown near the feeding centre or shipped in from elsewhere, or stored residues of arable crops, or fodder trees and shrubs for use as emergency fodder... Two or three times in every five years a drought in the pre-Saharan zone causes great losses, and every 20 years there is a catastrophic drought which causes an 80 per cent loss of livestock. In the severe winter of 1953–54, losses among flocks not associated with the these centres amounted to up to 40 per cent of adult sheep and 80 per cent of the lambs, whereas losses where such centres existed were not more than 15 per cent for the private owners and 3 per cent for the flocks belonging to the centres.[2]

Some idea of the far-reaching problems involved in an attempt to improve semi-arid grazing land can be obtained from the following list of proposed duties and responsibilities of the Range Division within the Ministry of Agriculture for Iraq:

1. To establish a system of administration and management for the proper use and improvement of the range and its forage, soil, and water resources. Range districts may be established so that ownership and use patterns may be improved so that grazing use may be made orderly and stable, and so that programmes for stocking the range with livestock may be made more consistent with the preventing of deterioration and the improving of range productivity.
2. To assist tribal groups and others utilizing the range to adopt more stable settlements so that the range may be better used and so that schools, roads and other public services may be more effectively provided.
3. To survey the range areas to ascertain the present condition of each area, and to determine the proper kind and number of livestock pastured and the seasons when the range may best be used.
4. To determine where water spreading may be most effectively undertaken, to construct and put into operation demonstration water-spreading projects and to advise and assist suitable groups or individuals to undertake such programmes.
5. To conduct programmes of demonstration of revegetation of the range for the establishment of desirable native or introduced grasses, shrubs, legumes or other plants and to arrange for the production of seed or plants where this is considered necessary or desirable, and to consult, advise and assist groups in the revegetation of the ranges. Provided also, that where it is distinctly in the public interest, noxious or undesirable plants may be controlled or eradicated.
6. To co-operate closely with the Ministries of Development and the Interior to determine the need for and the proper location of proposed new wells in the range areas, and to develop a system of control and use of such wells which will contribute best to the preservation or improvement of the range.
7. To establish or construct such test areas, fenced plots, pastures and experimental ranges as may be necessary to test or demonstrate ways and means of utilizing, preserving or improving the range.
8. To make observations and to advise the Minister on the status and needs of the wild-life which is dependent upon the ranges and which is an important national resource.
9. To recommend to the Minister from time to time the need for undertaking other activities in the interest of preserving and improving the range.[3]

Although some variant of commercial grazing is at present the only effective way of utilizing huge areas of semi-desert, this type of farming

---

[2] B. T. Dickson (ed.), op. cit., p. 165.

[3] Iraq, Ministry of Agriculture, 'Act for the improvement of the range (draft)', Baghdad, 1955.

remains at best marginal and at worst precarious. A successful reclamation scheme brings its own dangers, for a series of good years and increased productivity tends to entice farmers to increase the numbers of their livestock beyond the safety margin, so leading to renewed overgrazing and the certainty of ruin during a severe drought. Thus any future extension of arid-land grazing will need to be most carefully planned and controlled.

7. The humid temperate lands

Well-watered temperate lands include some of the world's most valuable farming country, notably in western Europe, south-east Australia, New Zealand and eastern North America. Even so, each of these regions contains extensive areas which are at present little used or even completely neglected, and which could be made agriculturally productive. Even larger areas await fuller exploitation in Uruguay and southern Brazil. In Europe the main types of marginal farmland are (i) badly drained uplands, for example the hill-peat country of central Wales and the Belgian Ardennes; (ii) badly drained lowlands, for example the peat bogs of central Ireland and the Pripet Marshes in west European Russia and (iii) sandy heathlands, such as the Campine of Belgium and the Landes in south-west France.

Hill reclamation. Many upland farms in north-west Europe include patches of un-reclaimed mixed heath or bog, often surrounded by cultivated fields. These patches sometimes mark terrain which has been especially difficult to reclaim, and sometimes land which has once been brought under cultivation but has been allowed to revert to waste. Examples of the latter are widespread in Ireland, where the disastrous famines of the 1840s eased pressure on the land and triggered off a century of emigration. Similar patches are easily identifiable on the edge of Dartmoor (*see photo*) and are commonplace in Brittany. Research by the Welsh Plant Breeding establishment at Aberystwyth has also established that in the early 19th century oats were grown on selected parts of the Welsh hills up to 450 m–520 m: these fields, long since abandoned, are today distinguished by the better pasture they yield. The existence of these modified pastures suggests that a further 400 000 ha of rough hill pasture in Wales could be similarly improved. Many of the predominant natural grasses provide inferior fodder for sheep, being unpalatable like *Nardus*, deficient in lime or other nutrients like *Agrostis* and *Festuca*, or only available briefly each year like the deciduous *Molinia*. The hill pastures also lack leguminous plants such as white clover and nutritious herbs such as daisies.

Fields reverting to waste on edge of Dartmoor at Oke-hampton.

Even by the simple process of cutting off, grazing hard and then manuring, the bent and fescue, i.e. the better grasses, are increased in numbers; thus large areas of our hill pastures can easily be improved. The method is to fire, then to prepare the surface by disc-ploughs drawn by tractors, then to manure with basic slags and nitrate chalk, and then to scatter seeds over the surface, especially of wild white clover. Actually the ploughing, manuring, seeding and rolling can be done in one operation, the necessary implements being drawn by one tractor. It may be necessary to distribute small quantities of soil from lowland regions which is inoculated with the nitrogen-fixing bacteria required for the life of a leguminous plant such as clover. Surface sowing of these hill pastures is possible because of the extreme moisture of the climate.[1]

Heather-clad moorlands can also be improved by burning, the young heather shoots providing especially nutritious feed for sheep. The pastures could be further improved by allowing limited numbers of cattle to feed on the moors, not as an economic proposition in themselves, but to enrich the soil with their valuable manure. Another suggestion is that trees should be planted as shelter belts so that sheep can be kept on the upland pastures throughout the year.

In Northern Ireland, where there has been considerable hill reclamation in recent years, drainage problems arise due to the presence in sandy podzols of hard-pans, often overlain by twentyfive or thirty centimetres of peat.[2] The hard-pan is broken up and turned in with the peat, but to do this special crawler tractors, heavy ploughs, disc harrows and rollers are necessary. Specially widened tracks on the tractors enable them to grip the wet spongy peat, and the ploughs can carve out a furrow forty-five centimetres deep. A cost problem arises because the heavy machinery has to be transported on special low-loading articulated trucks, and so reclamation is only economic if several adjacent patches are dealt with in the same locality. Soils on the newly reclaimed land are usually acidic and deficient in nitrates, and so lime is added together with nitrogenous and other fertilizers. Within two years the newly-won fields yield nutritious crops of fodder grasses.

[1] L. Dudley Stamp and S. H. Beaver, *The British Isles*, Longmans, p. 210.
[2] See Leslie Symons, 'Hill Reclamation in Northern Ireland', *Geography*, No. 197, on which the following account is based.

Reclaiming hill country in central Wales. A powerful crawler tractor hauling a specially designed plough through peaty ground. The deep furrows provide drainage channels. Later the land may be afforested or converted into cultivated pasture.

Another example of success in difficult conditions on the Tyrone flanks of the Sperrin Hills is a large field with a strike of good grasses cut out of the bog at 700 to 800 feet altitude six years ago. Such reclamation was once carried on laboriously by spade labour, rigging the land and planting with potatoes, a fraction of an acre at a time. Now the initial cultivations can be carried out over a large field in a few days and so far nearly 4520 acres have been reclaimed, This is equal to only about 1 per cent of the total acreage in rotation in the two counties, but the addition to the improved acreage of individual farms is often 20 per cent or more.[3]

Hill reclamation of this kind is expensive, and in Northern Ireland up to 50 per cent of the cost is borne by the Government, which also makes available the special machinery.

Many remote uplands in north-west Europe suffer from several generations of rural depopulation and a general deficiency of material and social amenities. Where, as in the Highlands of Scotland, attempts have been made to remedy these shortcomings by providing more housing, piped water, grid electricity, schools, better roads and transport facilities, there is often an accompanying effort at land reclamation. Even so, by its very nature hill-land must remain marginal land, and it is impossible to generalize on the

[3] Leslie Symons, loc. cit.

possibilities for its reclamation. The decision whether to reclaim hill-land in the face of a rigorous-climate, a short growing season, poor drainage, thin soils, isolation and a depressed rural society depends on the precise local environment and on the national farming policy.

Lowland bog reclamation. Vast areas of land in temperate latitudes, notably in the northern hemisphere, are smothered beneath marsh or bog. The soils in these areas contain excess water, but the presence of peat does not necessarily mean that reeds, rushes and mosses represent a region's climax vegetation. This is because much existing peat, especially in north-west Europe, was formed just after the Ice Age, when the climate was wetter and cooler than it is today. Much of this 'fossil' peat is now in the process of decay and, together with true living bogs, can be drained and converted into productive farmland or forest. Bogs form on virtually any land, but many European bogs are developed on potentially fertile boulder clays, loess and lake-silts, as well as on solid formations such as

---

REGIONS WITH MUCH RECLAIMABLE
BOG

Scandinavia
Finland
N. and W. European Russia
Ireland
Western Siberia

---

the Weald and Gault Clays. Most of these boggy soils are rich in both organic and inorganic plant nutrients, for their waterlogged condition prevents leaching. Drainage improves the crumb structure of soils and makes them easier to cultivate; it also makes them more fertile by allowing entry into the ground of aerobic bacteria. Two types of drainage are necessary: (i) open ditches to remove surface water and (ii) underground pipes or tunnels (excavated by a mole plough) to drain the soil. The reclaimed land is then further improved by adding lime to reduce soil acidity, and fertilizers.

Large-scale drainage schemes are at present being carried out over an enormous area of the Soviet Union. All of the regions involved have a relatively low annual rainfall of 500 mm– 750 mm, but evaporation rates are low due to the cold winters, cool summers and frequently cloudy skies. Apart from true bogland, with its characteristic covering of small trees, bushes, sedges, reeds and coarse grasses, large areas would be much improved by drainage, even though they are at present being used for cultivation or pasture. Altogether over 1·6 million square kilometres of land are involved, mostly in the Baltic Republics, north-west Russia, north-west Ukraine, the Pripet Marshes of Belorussia and the West Siberian Lowlands. Virtually all of the West Siberian Lowlands and about 20 per cent of the other territories need drainage, including much land in the west which has once been drained but which now requires re-draining. The reclaimed areas are used mainly to produce fodder crops such as sown grasses, oats, barley, green-maize and roots. The principal products from the livestock which these crops support are liquid milk and pig-meat.

During the past century there has also been extensive reclamation of bogland in the Scandinavian States and Finland, where expanding populations have exerted increasing pressures on limited land resources. The Governments of these countries from time to time sponsor reclamation campaigns and provide financial and other benefits for farmers wishing to reclaim waste land. In addition many voluntarily organized groups, e.g. the Swedish Peat Society, encourage reclamation as a patriotic duty. Examples of notable achievements include the constant enlargement of the cultivated area along the coastal plain of Finland, the draining of 5 m deep quaking bogs in interior Finland and Sweden, and extensive reclamation of peaty areas at Vildmose (near Aalborg) in Denmark, As in Norway and Flahult (near Jönköping) in Sweden. In Sweden the drained peat mosses of northern Norrland are cultivated in 4-hectare farm plots, the farmers obtaining a subsidiary income from forestry. Farther south the reclaimed bogland provides the sole livelihood for farmers on plots of 12 hectares.

Another country with massive drainage problems is Ireland, where peatbogs cover about 1·2 million hectares of the 7 million hectares of the Republic. The major Irish bogs are located in the Central Plain, where peat has accumulated at low levels as a result of impeded drainage rather than high rainfall. As these bogs are large, deep and relatively accessible they have become a major focus of bog utilization schemes in

Western Europe. In particular the Irish have pioneered the development of peat-fired electricity generating stations. This novel form of bog utilization is only economic, however, on the larger bogs which comprise rather less than one-half of the total badly drained area of the Central Plain. The remaining smaller bogs are being reclaimed for agriculture or forestry, an example being the development of Gowla bog in eastern Galway by the Irish Sugar Company.

... this company bought 1000 acres of Gowla bog ... to reclaim it for the growth of sugar beet; later, another 1300 acres were added. The project was undertaken with the object of supplying beet to the company's factory at Tuam, some 30 miles away. It takes 200 000 acres of beet a season to keep the factory in production, but nothing like this acreage has ever been grown locally, and in the past a costly diversion of beet from the main factory at Carlow has been necessary. The development of Gowla bog is taking place in small sections. Draining the first of these took two years and was made partly to pay for itself by the use of peat cut from the ditches as fuel for the Tuam factory. A grass-drying plant has been erected on the edge of the bog and peat from ditching now fires this also. The drained parts of the bog are dressed with ground limestone, potash, rock phosphate and copper sulphate down to a depth of 8 inches, and a mixture of timothy grass and clover is then sown to create a depth of soil sufficient for sugar beet (each crop of grass produces about 4 inches of new soil). In addition, peppermint and spearmint have been grown for export to the United States and sheep and bullocks grazed on the erstwhile bog to help defray development costs. The growing of sugar beet begins when a 2-foot depth of soil has been created, and a rotation of two years of grasses to one beet crop has been adopted for the small area so far brought to this stage.[1]

Such schemes are costly and are only worth while if the reclaimed land is used intensively and is heavily fertilized each year. It is possible to grow only a limited range of crops, of which grass is the most important, and during an unusually damp year flooding can seriously interrupt grazing. After about ten years of cropping and fertilizing the reclaimed peat can

[1] D. W. Dwyer, 'The Peat Bogs of the Irish Republic: A Problem in Land Use', *Geographical Journal*, Vol. CXXVIII, Part 2.

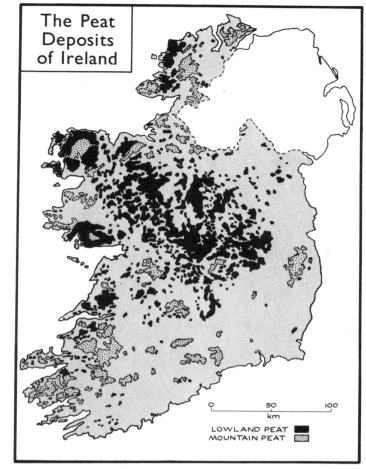

The Peat Deposits of Ireland

LOWLAND PEAT ■
MOUNTAIN PEAT ▨

support a grass ley for several years running, but thereafter rotation with other crops is needed more frequently than on other soils. Fodder crops of oats and barley provide good yields but are costly to produce because specially adapted machines are needed to cope with the the spongy ground. Farming costs are raised, too, by the need to plant shelter belts of trees: these cut down the force of the driving winds and rain

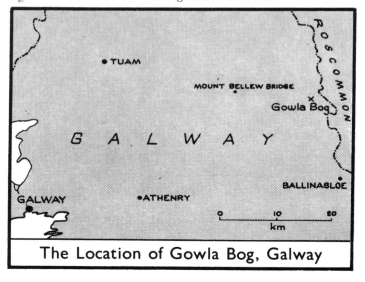

The Location of Gowla Bog, Galway

during wet 'Atlantic' weather and protect the peaty soils from dusting and wind erosion during occasional dry spells. In an attempt to widen the farming possibilities experiments are in progress with industrial crops such as bamboo (for wood-pulp), New Zealand flax and hemp (for fibres) and potatoes (for starch and industrial alcohol).

Although many boggy soils are very productive when drained, serious difficulties can arise with the reclaimed land. The problem of wind erosion of dusty peat soils is referred to above. A greater danger is that of flooding, for the draining of peat greatly increases the run-off. Water channels must therefore be enlarged so that they can handle at least twice their pre-drainage capacity. Even so, it may well prove difficult to dispose of the increased run-off because gradients in marshy areas are usually slight. Flood dangers are increased, too, by the gradual collapse in the level of reclaimed peat due to shrinkage and solution. Peat deposits consist almost entirely of plant remains, and these persist almost unchanged as long as the ground remains water-logged. Following drainage, however, the peat is attacked by bacteria, decomposes into soluble debris and is carried away in solution: the level of the land therefore falls. In the English Fenland

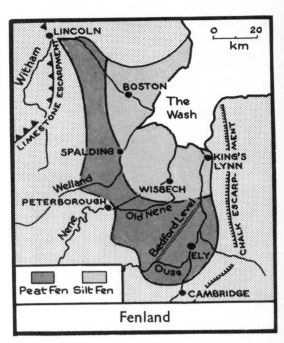

Fenland

(*see map*) the level of the drained peat has fallen to such an extent that it is now 3 metres lower than the inorganic silty marshlands adjacent to the Wash. Prior to draining the peat stood about 1·8 metres higher than the silt. (*See also photo.*)

The cultivated Fens are thus well below sea-level at every high tide and are constantly getting lower as more and more peat disintegrates. The problem is exacerbated by the fact that peat along the rivers and drains remains waterlogged and unaffected, so that all the main water-courses now flow well above the general level of the cultivated land; this increases the danger in times of flood and also necessitates all the water from the field drains being pumped up to a higher level. Diesel engines now work the pumps day and night; a complicated system of locks and sluices keep back the sea at high tide and permit outward drainage at low tide.. . . In fen peat we thus have an example of a natural soil which cannot possibly survive improvement and cultivation. Its innate fertility has led farming communities and larger organizations to devote vast resources to its initial drainage but, when once this has been achieved, its complete destruction is ultimately assured.[1]

Heathland develops in wet temperate latitudes, mainly on gravelly or coarse sandy soils. In Britain, for example, there are heaths on the

[1] S. R. Eyre, *Vegetation and Soils*, Edward Arnold, p. 190.

Holme Post, Huntingdonshire. In 1848 this post was driven into the Fenland peat so that its top was flush with ground level. This photograph indicates the remarkable change in level of the drained peat fen since that date.

Bagshot Beds of the London Basin, the Lower Greensand escarpments of the Weald and the Jurassic sandstones of Lincoln Edge and the North York Moors. The typical heathland soils are podzols, with a strongly leached horizon containing virtually no plant nutrients (*see photo*). A metre or so below the surface there is often a hard-pan of ferruginous salts which impedes drainage and gives rise to local peat bogs. The predominant heathland plant is heather (ling), but many other plants may be present including bilberry, coarse grasses, dwarf birches, conifers and bracken. Heathlands essentially similar to those in Britain are found on the glacial and riverine sands and gravels of the Netherlands and Belgium, the North German Plain and the Jutland peninsula in Denmark. Similar heath formations also occur in European Russia, Poland, temperate North America and in the southern hemisphere.

In their natural condition heathlands are infertile and virtually worthless, but large-scale reclamation followed the pioneer efforts of Norfolk landowners in the late 18th century. Sheep were folded on the land to add valuable manure, and the famous 'Norfolk Four-Course System' was introduced. This involves a crop rotation of wheat, turnips, barley and clover, and enables bacteria in nodules on the clover roots to 'fix' nitrogen from the air and so eventually enrich the soil with nitrogenous salts. Chemical fertilizers are added to provide phosphates and potash, and the soil is limed to reduce its acidity. Variations of the Norfolk System have been applied with considerable success on heathlands in Europe. In the Netherlands, for example, manure is dug into the sands, together with the organic waste from town garbage collections, and the improved land is used to grow good crops of potatoes, rye, oats and sugar beet. Recently an average of 5000 hectares of sandy heath has been reclaimed in the Netherlands each year. Heathland pastures are also improved, notably in the Campine of Belgium, where special quick-growing, drought-resistant and tenacious root-binding grasses have been evolved by the Ministry of Agriculture Research Institution. The table overleaf shows the spectacular progress in heathland reclamation in Jutland, following the formation in 1866 of the Danish Heath Society. In West Germany only about one-quarter of the former 7000 square kilometres of the Lüneburg

(Above) Podzol in a sandy heath, Surrey. Note the thin layer of humus, whitish leached horizon and darker lower zone, all of which typify this type of soil.

(Below) Heathland, central Jutland.

Heath remains, and the largest tract of *continuous* heath there now measures only 36 square kilometres.[1]

There is no doubt that *all* remaining heathland could be reclaimed, but it is questionable whether it would be advantageous to do so. It has long been realized that money spent on improving superior land brings in a greater return than the expenditure of the same amount on heathland soils, and recent technical improvements in such matters as drainage, fertilizers and cultivation tend to widen this differential. Another complication is the fact that heathland provides pleasant open country for recreation and it may be felt that such facilities should be preserved in spite of the potential gain in foodstuffs which reclamation would make available.

Reclamation of tidal swamp and portions of the sea-bed has in some countries added significantly to the area available for farming. The most notable example is the Netherlands, where no less than two-fifths of the entire country was once under sea-water. Other noteworthy areas include: the Belgian maritime polders near Antwerp; the West German coast from the Dollard to the Elbe estuary (the *märschen*); portions of the Camargue in southern France; the Pontine Marshes of the Italian Maremma and, in Britain, the silt fen adjacent to the Wash, the former Wantsum Channel in east Kent, Romney Marsh and the Somerset Fens. Generally speaking these reclaimed areas provide very fertile and productive farmland: in the famous North-east Polder of the Netherlands, for example, 98 per cent of the soils is classified as 'very good'. In fact the soils on polderland vary considerably, including heavy marine clays, peats, sands and silts, and land-use patterns reflect these soil differences. Thus the heavier clays and peats are converted into permanent

1 See Dickinson, *Germany*, Methuen, p. 207.

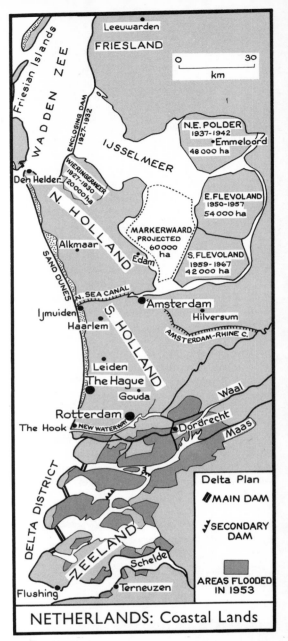

NETHERLANDS: Coastal Lands

pasture for livestock farming; the lighter marine clays and silt loams provide very valuable arable land and the sandier soils, when improved by digging in manure, marl and fertilizers, are excellent for market gardening.

The reclamation of the former Zuider Zee is the classic example of this method of gaining extra land for farming: details of this epic scheme are given above and overleaf. Various proposals have been put forward for other large

68

schemes of this type. For example, the Dutch are studying the feasibility and expense of reclaiming the shallow Wadden Zee. This could be done by sealing the gaps between the Friesian Islands and the mainland, and between the Islands themselves (*see map*). There are similar possibilities for reclamation on many other lowlands coasts with broad, shallow, lagoon-like indentations: examples include the Wash, the Baltic *haffen* and the lagoon-fringed coast of the southeastern U.S.A. As with all marginal lands the decision whether or not to reclaim depends ultimately on the cost of a scheme in relation to its potential benefits.

Coniferous forests (*taïga*) stretch almost without interruption across the sub-polar latitudes of North America and Eurasia. These forests already provide an enormous supply of softwood timber, notably in Canada, Sweden, Finland and North European Russia, but it has been estimated that in addition about 10 per cent of the forest land could be cultivated, and an even larger area reclaimed for pastoral farming. The largest area of reclaimable taïga lies in the Soviet Union, where considerable experimental farming and research has been carried out in recent decades. The physical geography of the taïga inhibits agriculture for a variety of reasons, the most significant of which are:

(i) **The very severe winter and short growing season.** Snow covers the land for about 250 days along the Arctic fringe of Siberia. The climate statistics at Yakutsk, an important centre of Soviet taïga experimental farming, are as follows:

°C.	−43	−36	−22	−8	6	16	19	14	6	−8	−20	−40	Total
R.f. mm	22·9	5·1	10·2	15·2	27·9	53·3	43·2	66·0	30·5	35·6	15·2	22·9	348·0

(ii) **The massive drainage problems.** The soil over much of the taïga remains excessively moist for long periods each year, despite the comparatively light precipitation. In spring this is due to snow melt, whilst in the summer and autumn it results from the falling of seasonal convectional rain (*see above*). In the centre and northern portions of the forest belt the sun's heat is sufficient to evaporate only between one-third and one-half of the annual precipitation. Thus poor surface drainage, accentuated by the remarkable flatness of much of the taïga, is a really fundamental problem.[1] Waterlogging prevents proper aeration of the topsoil, reduces the number of soil bacteria (thus hindering the evolution of humus), reduces the effectiveness of chemical fertilizers and encourages the formation of strongly leached, infertile podzols. The podzols in turn develop hard-pans (*see p.* 67), which further impedes drainage and leads to the formation of peat bogs. The salts within a hard-pan are not easily assimilated by plants, and often include compounds of aluminium and iron which are positively harmful.

(iii) **The widespread occurrence of boulders and stones** derived from glacial drift. Virtually all of the taïga was formerly covered by ice and it has been estimated[2] that in West European Russia alone no less than 1041 *million* tonnes of stones need to be removed from reclaimable forest soils. These stones are used for building farmhouses, roads and railways, but a large proportion are buried on the spot in specially dug drainage trenches, 'stone drains' of this type proving both effective and cheap.

When draining portions of the taïga the Russians have found that large open ditches are not satisfactory, for they hinder effective cultivation of the land by large-scale machinery. To combat waterlogging, Soviet methods

... combine the laying out of a sparse network of permanent open ditches with other methods of removing surplus water. One of these methods is ploughing along the slope combined with the laying out of transversal drain furrows that send the water into the sparse network of permanent ditches. Another means consists in mole draining and discharging the water into temporary transversal ditches which direct it into a sparse network

[1] It should be noted, however, that towards the southern edge of the taïga rainfall becomes deficient: here evaporation just about balances precipitation, the rainfall tends to be irregular and there are occasional droughts.

[2] Academician A. A. Grigoryev, 'The Reclamation of the Forest Belt of the U.S.S.R. in Europe', *Geographical Journal*, CXIX, p. 411.

There are several stages in the formation of marine polder-land. The sea-bed to be reclaimed is first sealed off with a ring-dyke. Photo **A** shows a length of such a dyke being built in the former Zuider Zee. Its foundations consist of huge quantities of clay, sand and silt dredged from the nearby sea floor. The sides of the dyke are open to erosion by currents and tidal scour, and they are protected by mattresses (photo **B**), formerly of interwoven willow boughs, now of nylon. These are secured to the clay by stakes, and weighted by thousands of stones.

The top layer of stones is carefully faced with concrete or basalt blocks (photo **C**). If the top of the dyke is sandy, marram grass may be planted and fences built to prevent the sand being blown away (photo **D**). When the ring-dyke is complete, the water inside is pumped out. In the past the pumps were driven by windmills, but today they are mostly powered by steam or diesel engines.

When a marine polder is first pumped dry its soil contains much salt. This is removed within about four years by being dissolved by rain water and then pumped away. Deep ploughing (photo **E**) improves the soil, and if it is planted with crops the polder will soon look like the one in photo **G**. This is part of the Great North-East Polder (map page 68). Look closely and you will see the outline of the former island of Schokland, now entirely surrounded by fertile farmland. Photo **F** shows the island before reclamation began.

Polders with soils consisting of sea-clay are extremely fertile and are intensely cultivated with such crops as cereals, sugar-beet, vegetables and flowers. The peaty alluvial polders are less fertile and are mostly put down in permanent grass-land for dairying.

of permanent ditches. The network of perm-anent open ditches is so arranged in these cases that they lie 10–20 hectares apart, which makes is possible to apply machinery. In a number of cases this system of drainage has to be applied as a temporary measure even on areas where, later on, the creation of a thick loose arable and sub-arable layers will be quite sufficient. The creation of a thick loose layer is often impossible without a preliminary draining of the land.[1]

The drained taïga podzols are then enriched by adding chemical fertilizers, dung enriched with superphosphates, and peat and dung composts. The improved soils are then well suited to forage, vegetable, grass and green silage crops. Soviet experiments show that the taïga becomes cultivable if a minimum depth of 30 cm of well-drained topsoil is prepared, for this can absorb up to 50 mm of summer rain without becoming waterlogged. In the event of drought the wet soil below this depth will supply moisture to plant roots by upward capillary movements, triggered off by evaporation from the ground surface.

An interesting aspect of Soviet taïga reclama-tion is the deliberate retention of forests, especially of larch, alongside the newly-won fields. The trees serve a number of useful pur-poses, mainly in relation to drainage. For example, their presence reduces the run-off, for much moisture is transpired through their leaves. By casting deep shade the trees also retard snow-melt, and this in turn eases the burden of rivers during the spring floods and replenishes them during the low-water period of late summer. As well as reducing the danger of flooding the more even flow of the rivers also favours navigation and the generation of hydro-electricity for rural communities. Furthermore the trees provide shelter for growing crops and stabilize the looser, sandy podzols, thus reducing wind and water erosion.

On the reclaimed taïga of eastern Siberia there are some remote agricultural settlements which provide foodstuffs for communities of miners, lumbermen, hunters and fishermen. The most

notable sub-polar farmlands, however, are at Yakutsk (62° N.), where, over a period of many years

> the Russians have developed strains of wheat, barley and rye that in some cases mature within 60 days after planting.[2]

Considering the shortness of the summer and the relatively low precipitation (*see p.* 69) this is a remarkable achievement. However, the short summers are hot (even melons can be grown) and it is thought that moisture seeps up to the topsoil from the deep-seated layer of permafrost. The total area of arable land around Yakutsk is not very large, about the size of a small English county. The main emphasis lies on raising cattle, as it does too at Syktyvkar (64° N.), another Soviet high-latitude farming community in the Komi Republic. According to Soviet scientists[3] there are great opportunities for expanding live-stock farming, especially dairying, in the region around Syktyvkar. Sufficient hay and silage can be obtained in summer to provide for a long period of stall-feeding of up to 250 days.

To be really suitable for agricultural develop-ment an area of taïga must possess a com-bination of special advantages such as a south-facing aspect, soils which are less leached than usual or are alluvial, or a favourable location in relation to river or rail transport. One very promising region of the Soviet taïga is the middle Lena Valley,

> where soil and vegetation conditions are comparable with those in patches of wooded steppe and steppe several hundred miles south, and even chernozem-like soils occur.[4]

Research into the agricultural potential of the taïga, very similar to that outlined above in the U.S.S.R., is being carried out in North America, notably in the Peace River country of Canada, and at Fairbanks, Alaska (65° N.). Indeed most of the strains of quick-growing, hardy cereals being tested at Fairbanks came originally from Yakutsk.

1 Academician A. A. Grigoryev, loc. cit.

2 Cole and German, *A Geography of the U.S.S.R.*, Butter-worths.

3 E.g. Chertdantsev G. N. (ed.), *Ekon. Geog. S.S.S.R.*, 1958, 'Zones of Agricultural Specialization of the U.S.S.R.' pp. 206–40.

4 Cole and German, op. cit.

Section III. **Possibilities of intensifying world agriculture**

So far in this book we have been concerned mainly with possibilities of extending the world's total cultivated area. Now we must consider ways in which agricultural methods can be improved and intensified, so that each hectare of existing farmland is made to yield its maximum food potential. At present only a small proportion of the world's arable and pastoral farmlands is intensively farmed in this way, and it will be shown that there exist possibilities for a massive increase in farm output, especially in the economically underdeveloped regions of the world. These possibilities will be discussed under the following headings: Control of Soil and Water; Plant and Animal Breeding; Control of Pests and Diseases; Mechanization and Equipment; Storage, Handling and Processing Methods; Land-holding and Management.

8. Control of soil and water

Good soil and an adequate water supply are both fundamental preliminaries in any attempt to raise agricultural yields. The nature, fertility and continued well-being of a soil are all intimately affected by the water which passes across and through it, and so it is convenient to link together a study of Man's use and misuse of soil and water.

The problem of soil erosion is now well documented[5] and understood in all advanced farming societies, mainly as a result of protests and warnings made during the past few decades by geographers and agronomists. Even so there are enormous areas, notably in the southern hemisphere, where little if any attempt is made to halt the deterioration of soils by bad farming practices. The result is that farming yields are much lower than need be, and large areas of land are continually being lost by misuse. Common faults include shifting cultivation, overgrazing, the wholesale destruction of forests, growing the same crop year after year and not using manures or fertilizers. The deterioration of the soil which inevitably results from such malpractices can lead to its destruction by wind-, sheet- and gully-erosion.

Wind-erosion is most likely to occur on flat or gently undulating land where the soils are light and are prone to disintegrate during dry weather. Sandy and reclaimed peaty soils are especially vulnerable because they lack an admixture of clay to bind the surface particles together. During a dry spell the top few centimetres of such soils break down into a fine dust, especially where it has been finely prepared to form seed-beds for such crops as sugar beet and turnips. Where there is no marked relief to break the force of the wind, the surface soil is swept off to a depth of seven to ten centimetres. This happens frequently, for example, in the English Fenlands, where drainage ditches and drains become choked with wind-blown soil particles.

Not only the topsoil is removed, for sometimes newly tilled seeds and even small plants are blown bodily from the fields. As wind-erosion is most likely to occur in the Fenlands during the planting months of April and May[6] it is not uncommon for a farmer to have to reseed a single field several times in one season.

When soil is affected by blowing it is the more fertile particles of humus and fine clay which are the first to disappear. In time virtually all the 'goodness' is removed and only heavy, infertile

5 See, e.g., Jacks and Whyte, *The Rape of the Earth*. Fairfield Osborne, *Our Plundered Planet*.

6 Brade-Birks, *Good Soil*, E.U.P., p. 183, 'When blowing occurs it is usually in April or May—the season is remarkably constant. Once the soil has dried out before the crops cover the ground erosion is liable to occur.'

Wind erosion stripping soil from a maize field in Iowa.

grains of quartz remain. As well as causing erosion the blowing of soil particles can also spread plant pests and diseases, as eggs, bacteria and spores are carried from field to field. Wind-erosion on a devastating scale afflicted the drier parts of the North American prairies during the 1930s. Encouraged by a succession of wet years, and enticed by the prospect of making quick profits, farmers had ploughed up thousands of square miles of semi-arid grassland and converted the landscape into a 'golden ocean' of wheat. Then came, inevitably, a series of dry seasons, and so the newly-won fields were turned into a vast parched, dust-strewn, uncultivable wilderness. Thousands of farmers were forced to abandon their land in a 'Dust Bowl' which

An approaching soil dust-storm in Colorado.

reached hundreds of kilometres through the States of Colorado, Kansas, Texas and Oklahoma, and northwards into Saskatchewan and Alberta. The misery and desperation which ensued are powerfully portrayed in Steinbeck's famous novel *The Grapes of Wrath*.

There had been periods of drought before the 'thirties but they never had lasted for so long or been so severe. Fields a mile square that had yielded Number 1 Hard wheat were transformed into dunes of wind-blown top-soil, anchored only when rolling tumbleweed piled it along fences or withered hedges of carragana. Families once happy and hopeful moved away destitute. Farms were abandoned. Here and there appeared what became the tragic symbol of those unhappy times, the Bennett Buggy, named in derision of the Prime Minister of the day, an old car drawn by a team (of horses) because its owner could not afford to buy gasoline. Yet, despite the appalling desolation, not everyone was hopeless. The prairies would come back, men said . . . and bravely they sang their parody of *Beulah Land*:

> We sit and gaze across the plains
> And wonder why it never rains.[1]

It 'never' rained for the simple reason that the climate of the interior prairies is semi-arid, with a rainfall that fluctuates widely from year to year, both in its total and in its distribution. Much of the land in the 'Dust Bowl' should never have been put under the plough, and some of it has reverted to permanent pasture. Elsewhere a variety of conservation techniques makes it possible to till the semi-arid prairie without fear of wind-erosion. Irrigation water, sprayed over the ground by sprinklers, keeps the topsoil damp and stops it collapsing into dust; specially aligned fences and shelter belts of trees reduce the force and impact of the wind; weeds are encouraged to grow so that as little of the topsoil as possible is exposed to the air. Above all, the land is cultivated by rotation in strips, entailing a 'patchwork-quilt' of cultivated and non-cultivated fields (*see photo*): this method ensures that no large areas of soil are ever exposed for long to the effects of the wind, and any dust picked up from the bare patches is trapped by the adjacent plants. The map shows that shelter belts are now a recognized method of cultivation

1 M. J. Campbell, *The Face of Canada*, Harrap, p. 153.

Irrigated land on the Canterbury Plains, New Zealand. The strategic planting of coniferous wind-breaks reduces the risk of serious wind erosion in this rain-shadow zone.

in the drier steppes of the Soviet Union: it is thought, however, that in spite of all precautions, widespread wind-erosion does from time to time occur in the 'Virgin Lands' of Soviet Central Asia. For example, dust storms of fine topsoil, borne aloft by easterly winds, were reported from many cities of eastern Europe during the summer of 1962.

Sheet-erosion results from an excessive moistening of soil particles and involves the removal of a more or less uniform depth of soil from a sloping field. After prolonged rainfall each minute particle of soil acquires a 'skin' of moisture which appears to act as a lubricant. The tiny soil grains thus gradually float and slip downhill under the force of gravity. Soil movements of this type are difficult to detect, for there is no obvious surface flow. In time, however, a farmer finds to his dismay that much of the topsoil has slithered away from the upper parts of his fields, which gradually lose their fertility. In Western Europe sheet-erosion is especially slow because the crumb structure of most European soils make them resistant to surface wash. Even so, the results of sheet-erosion are readily apparent on the steeply sloping fields of wetter regions such as south-west England. In Cornwall, for example, massive granite 'hedges' act as barriers to soil which has flowed downhill, so that the height of a hedge on the uphill side may be only a few inches, whereas it is several feet on the downhill side (*see diagram A*). Sheet-erosion is also accentuated by *solifluction*, i.e. the slipping of topsoil downhill during a thaw, when there is melt-water present in the top few centimetres of the ground but the deeper soil remains frozen solid (*diagram B*). Solifluction occurred on a massive scale in southern England during the Ice Age, with effects which are particularly noticeable on the coastal plain of West Sussex: the plain around Chichester is smeared with thousands of tonnes of chalky soil sludge which slid southwards off the dip-slope of the Downs.

Various measures may be taken to prevent sheet-erosion, notably contour ploughing, i.e. ploughing the land along the slope. This produces a pattern of horizontal furrows (*top photo*) which hinders the downhill flow of moistened topsoil. Contour ploughing also reduces soil erosion by cutting down the run-off and making the soil more absorbent. Large, gently inclined drainage ditches may also be cut, so that excess rain-water can move downhill in a controlled fashion, without spilling over and waterlogging the whole surface of the ground. In north-west Europe, where rainfall is usually gentle and is well distributed throughout the year, precautions of this kind are rarely practised: they are vital, however, in tropical and continental interior lands liable to heavy and repeated convectional downpours.

Gully-erosion can result if rain-water moves across bare soil along a clearly defined course. This may happen on arable land due to the topography, or because the land has been cultivated in a particular way. For example, the existence of ploughed furrows running straight down a steep slope provides runnels which, following a heavy rainstorm, can be transformed into dangerous water-filled gullies. Similar gullies may result if cattle constantly tread over the same patch of ground. Once a gully has become established it extends itself at an alarming speed by headward erosion and by developing tributary gullies. In a short space of time formerly productive farmland is devastated by a ramification of gullies as in lower photo opposite. The formation of gullies greatly increases the run-off, so that less water seeps into the soil, the water-table falls and the soil becomes less fertile. The decrease in surface water also reduces the cover of natural vegetation, and this in turn accentuates the run-off still further. Earlier this century this dismal cycle of events produced huge areas of useless 'badlands' in the western high plains of the U.S.A. The lower photograph shows farmland devastated by gully-erosion in Tennessee. Once gully-erosion has got a grip it is difficult to rectify, but the gullies can be blocked with earth, stone and concrete dams. These cause silt to accumulate and the gullies are gradually filled. At the same time bushes and grasses are planted on the slopes of the gullies to stabilize the soil.

The soil conservation methods outlined above can be remarkably effective. In Somalia, for

Soil Creep indicated by accumulation of soil against Cornish hedges

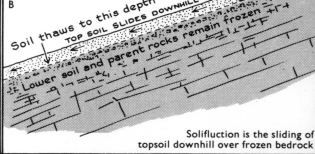

Solifluction is the sliding of topsoil downhill over frozen bedrock

Contour strip cultivation in Iowa. Ploughing and cultivating 'along the contour' reduces the risk of sheet erosion and gullying. Planting of alternate strips is a safeguard against wind-blowing of top soil.

Gully erosion in Tennessee.

example, a combination of earth banks, spillways and graded drainage channels

> can in a bad season make the difference between a crop and no crop, and in a good year can substantially increase the yield, while protecting the land from erosion. The system works almost automatically and requires only a minimum of maintenance.[1]

In Brazil

> mechanical practices, such as coffee planting on the contour and terracing, are now being widely used. Experimental work has indicated that the amount of soil lost yearly decreases from 2·2 tonnes to 0·29 tonnes per hectare where terraces are used. Even in contoured lands, the sandy soils, comprising most of the coffee area in São Paulo, are liable to erosion under the impact of driving torrential rains common to these areas. Efficient erosion control measures include the use of grass mulches. Contour ditches have been established in older plantations and coffee is planted on individual terraces on very steep hillsides. Strip weeding and the planting of contour hedges have also been carried out. This new phase of coffee production, based on good soil conservation practice, is becoming of increasing importance, not only to the large farms on recently deforested land in Parana but also on the rehabilitated older areas of coffee production. The tendency toward decrease in size of farms and gradual exhaustion of virgin soil will make these new techniques of intensive growing of paramount importance.[2]

There is, in fact, no place for complacency in these matters, for even in the U.S.A., where soil conservation techniques were first pioneered, there is still massive erosion. Since 1920 about 45 per cent of the original fertility of the land has been lost by water- and wind-erosion, overgrazing and overcropping. According to the United States Soil Service,

> soil losses by erosion from all lands in the United States total 5 400 000 000 tonnes annually. From farm lands alone, the annual loss is about 3 000 000 000 tonnes, enough to fill a freight train which would girdle the globe 18 times. . . . In a normal production year, erosion by wind and water removes 21 times

as much plant food from the soil as is removed in the crops sold off this land.

A new aspect of this difficult problem has recently become apparent in advanced countries, where modern cultivation machinery is so heavy that it compresses the wetter soils into an impermeable crust: this increases the run-off and so heightens the danger of sheet- and gully-erosion. This particular hazard might in the future be offset by using hovercraft.

To combat soil erosion on a regional scale a satisfactory balance must be achieved between the use of the land for arable, pastoral and forestry purposes. The situation as regards forests is often vital, because lack of tree cover can have the most serious effects. In the coffee-growing district of Brazil, for example, it has been shown that whereas there is an annual loss of 2 tonnes of soil per hectare where there is no vegetation cover, the loss on forested land is a mere 0·002 tonnes per hectare.[3] In such a case a carefully worked-out combination of forestry and arable farming does much to preserve the soil cover. In India the lack of trees not only accelerates soil erosion, crop desiccation and the encroachment onto fertile land of wind-blown sand, but also leads to the use of dung as a fuel, thereby reducing the amount of organic waste which is returned to help maintain soil fertility.

We have seen that one way in which erosion can be minimized is by controlling the movement of water over the surface of a soil. In addition, a careful check must be kept on the amount of water contained within a soil, if maximum crop yields are to be obtained. When it rains a proportion of the water which enters the soil drains down through and it lost, and the remainder is retained in the soil pores within a few feet of the ground surface. This retained or 'immovable' water is then available for growing crops, but plants cannot use the whole of it, for as more and more water is removed it becomes harder to extract. In humid regions such as the British Isles the roots of plants can exert a pull of up to about 10 atmospheres. Beyond that point, if no more rain falls, most plants will begin to wilt, even though the soil is still somewhat moist.[4] To

[1] Walter H. Pawley, op. cit.
[2] Walter H. Pawley, op. cit.

[3] Ibid.
[4] See Sir E. John Russell, The World of the Soil, Fontana, p. 59.

maintain plant growth it then becomes necessary to irrigate the land, but the exact amount which can be added varies according to circumstances. In arid regions, where water is naturally in very short supply, it may be possible to add only just sufficient water to prevent wilting. Ideally, however, sufficient water should be added to keep the plants as near as possible to a state of maximum transpiration, because many plants grow best under these conditions. Quite brief interruptions to a plant's transpiration can seriously injure its growth, and in recent years it has increasingly been realized that supplementary irrigation is often very beneficial, even in humid lands where rainfall is apparently adequate. A comparison of these two maps shows that during an average growing season (April–September) south-east England receives 150 mm–225 mm less rainfall than is likely to be transpired by growing crops. Farmers in Kent, Surrey and Sussex know from experience that in nine seasons out of ten moisture deficiency is likely to occur in at least one growing month. In a particularly dry summer, crops are likely to suffer serious moisture deficits of 300 mm or more over the whole of England to the south and east of a line linking Weymouth–Hereford–Hull. To counter this problem increasing numbers of farmers, notably those concerned with vegetable and fruit production, are using underground irrigation pipes and sprinklers.

Cow-dung 'cakes' being dried for use as fuel, West Pakistan.

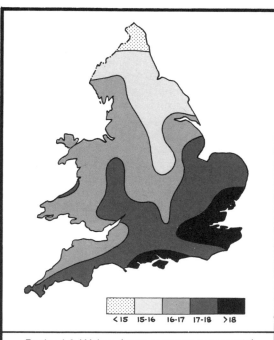

England & Wales: Average summer potential transpiration in inches. April–September[5]

< 15   15-16   16-17   17-18   >18

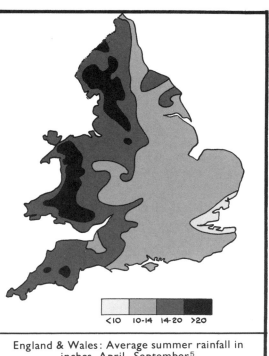

England & Wales: Average summer rainfall in inches. April–September[5]

< 10   10-14   14-20   >20

[5] Based on maps supplied by the Meteorological Office.

Sprinkler Irrigation. The photograph shows a new grass ley receiving sprinkler irrigation on a farm in Surrey. The pipes through which the water is being forced can easily be moved so that all of the field eventually gets a drenching.

Just how effective irrigation in England can be was demonstrated in the dry summer of 1955 when the average rainfall over the whole country in July was only 1·1 inch (27·9 mm) and

> . . . on the sandy soil at Woburn the addition of 6·3 ins. of water by irrigation . . . increased the yield of main crop potatoes from 11 tons to 20 per acre.[1]

Reports from the south-east U.S.A. show that the yields of such crops as seed cotton, tomatoes and beans are increased by two- or even three-fold by the use of periodic summer irrigation, and in Tennessee milk yields from irrigated pastures are improved by up to 43 per cent.[2]

In arid regions, where transpiration rates are highest, the amount of water needed to sustain plant growth is enormous. It has been estimated that

> . . . in a sub-tropical climate a tonne of maize can only be grown if 4000 tonnes of water are available for it.[3]

[1] Sir E. John Russell, op. cit., p. 221.

[2] 'Big Returns from Supplemental Irrigation', *Agricultural Research*, March, 1954, p. 14.

[3] Herbert Addison, *Land, Water and Food*, Chapman & Hall, p. 25.

On this basis a cultivated area of one square kilometre—i.e. an area about one-half the size of Hyde Park—requires 508 000 tonnes of water to produce about 125 tonnes of maize. The problem is aggravated by the massive evaporation in such regions, which greatly reduces the proportion of rain-water which actually enters the rivers: in the Murray River Basin of Australia, for example, it is less than 3 per cent. This is a major predicament for pastoral and arable farmers and for metropolitan water authorities, all of whom sustain heavy losses of water from reservoirs and open storage tanks. In South Australia various methods to counter seepage and evaporation from open reservoirs have recently been investigated, including the following:[4]

(*a*) The use of impervious plastic membranes to cover the bed of a lake. The membranes are kept in place by a 300 mm. layer of soil.

(*b*) Sealing a lake bed with (i) a chemical such as sodium tripolyphosphate, or (ii) a special clay—bentonite—imported from the U.S.A., or (iii) a soil cement, using a mixture of 10 per cent cement and 90 per cent soil.

(*c*) Covering the surface of a reservoir with a white, waxy film of insoluble hexadecanol (cetyl alcohol). The most effective way to spread

[4] G. Ross Cochrane, 'Reducing Water Loss in South Australia', *Geography*, No. 209.

hexadecanol is by blowing it as a fine powder through a tube from the stern of a moving boat. The cost is only one penny to save 4500 litres of water, and evaporation from large storage reservoirs is reduced by one-half.

Elsewhere, e.g. Cyrenaica, crop yields have been greatly increased by using prefabricated cement canals or pipelines instead of traditional earth ditches.

It has long been realized that the fertility of a soil can be improved by digging in organic substances such as human and animal excreta and vegetable composts. In China, where the art of manuring dates back to prehistoric times, soils are so revitalized with plant nutrients that many padi-fields have been in continuous cultivation for centuries.

About 85 per cent of the total cultivated area in China is manured, through organic manures such as night soil, stable manure, compost, green manure crops, mud from the bottom of canals and ponds rich in organic matter, oil cakes, etc. . . . It is estimated that some 50 per cent of the manure used is night soil and stable manure, 20 to 30 per cent compost and 10 to 15 per cent green manure. . . . Every effort is being made to utilize night soil and stable manure.[5]

Similar organic manures and composts are traditional in the great river flood-plains of the Middle East and their use spread to Europe with the Moorish invasions of the Middle Ages. In the 12th century a Moor called Ibn-al-Awam, who lived in Seville, wrote a *Book of Agriculture* in which he gave details of how to make compost. A pit should be dug and quantities of the following ingredients tipped in: excreta from humans, doves, asses and cows; powdered earth from below manure heaps; blood from human beings, camels and sheep; rain and other water. This recipe, though bizarre, is biologically sound. Since the 18th century it has also been known that crop rotations including grasses, legumes and cereals are another means of evolving more productive soils. This technique has greatly improved the fertility of farmland in north-western Europe, as have liming and the use of field drains. It was in Europe, too, that biologists first showed that the use of rotations, manures and composts improved the land because certain

[5] Report of the Indian Delegation to China on Agricultural Planning and Techniques.

minerals were thereby added to the soil. Details of these minerals which are vital to growing plants are listed in the table overleaf, together with information about their sources and nutritive effects.

Nowadays minerals are usually added in the form of chemical fertilizers (*see notes overleaf*). In many respect these are easier to apply and are more efficient than dressings of organic wastes. The content of modern chemical fertilizers can be minutely controlled, so that particular soil deficiencies can be rectified, or exact plant requirements supplied much more precisely than is possible when using composts or manure. In advanced countries the use of mineral fertilizers has increased enormously during the past fifty years (*see table*), with corresponding spectacular improvements in crop yields, but the vast

QUANTITIES OF FERTILIZERS USED BY FARMERS IN GREAT BRITAIN, EXPRESSED IN THOUSANDS OF TONS OF PLANT FOOD, IN VARIOUS YEARS.		
	NITROGEN	PHOSPHORIC ACID	POTASH
1900	16	110	7
1913	29	180	23
1929	48	198	52
1939	60	170	75
1946	165	358	120
1956	291	386	305
1968	451	363	407

majority of the world's farmlands still receive little or no dressing of any kind. In some backward rural communities there is the added complication that dried animal dung is used as a fuel and as a raw material for house construction. The photograph overleaf shows bricks being made from animal dung in an Indian village.

In India about 40 per cent of animal manure is used as a fuel for cooking and heating.

It has been argued that rock and synthetic fertilizers are in some way less valuable as plant nutrients than organic substances, as if the latter contained some vital life-giving element not present in inorganic chemicals. Recent research shows this to be untrue, nevertheless, there are certain dangers inherent in the sole use of chemicals over a long period of time. This practice apparently brings about complex chemical and physical changes in soils which cause a deteriora-

PRINCIPAL MINERALS ESSENTIAL TO PLANT GROWTH

A. Minerals which are required in considerable quantities.

Nitrates are commonly deficient in the wet, leached soils of north-west Europe and other humid temperate regions. They are particularly valuable in promoting the growth of wholesome green leaves in grasses and market garden crops such as cabbages, broccoli and lettuce. Large dressings of nitrate of ammonia are applied each spring to vegetables in such localities as Cornwall and the Channel Islands. During the 19th century very large quantities of nitrates were obtained from the 'caliche' beds of the Atacama Desert in northern Chile. These deposits are still worked, but their significance has been lessened by the availability of nitrates from other sources. One such source is ammonium sulphate, a by-product of the manufacture of coal-gas. Much more important is the massive production of ammonium nitrates via the fixation of nitrogen from the air. Nitrogen fixation by the Haber process requires an abundant supply of cheap electricity, which explains the location of nitrogenous fertilizer works in mountainous regions like Scandinavia, Switzerland and Quebec, where hydro-electricity is available.

Phosphates are particularly vital during the early stages of plant growth. They are often added to seed-beds where, by promoting root development, they encourage the growth of strong, healthy young plants, able to shake off disease. Root crops such as swedes, turnips and potatoes are particularly vulnerable to phosphate deficiencies. Phosphates were at one time mainly obtained from crushed bones. Nowadays supplies come from huge calcium phosphate quarries in North Africa, the U.S.A. and the U.S.S.R. The calcium phosphate is treated with sulphuric acid being marketed as 'superphosphate'. Additional supplies of phosphate are obtained by grinding up the basic slag of iron furnaces. An adequate supply of phosphates is vital in the development of the food resources of underdeveloped regions.

Potash is most likely to be deficient in sand, chalk and moorland soils, but clay may also require 'topping up' with this mineral. The crops most in need of potash are roots such as sugar beet, mangolds and potatoes, where its presence favours the formation of leaves with a large surface area. On the Rothamsted mangold field one ton of leaf produced 4·3 tons of roots when potassic fertilizer was supplied but only 2·9 tons where none was given.[1] Supplementary effects enable a plant more effectively to resist certain fungal diseases and a dry spell. Potash also improves the quality of straw in cereal crops and the quality of tree-fruits: it is much used, for example, in the apple orchards of Devon and Somerset and in the plum orchards of the Vale of Evesham.

Magnesium is an essential constituent of chlorophyll, the substance which absorbs sunlight and so enables a plant to build up organic materials by photosynthesis. A deficiency of magnesium causes leaves to become pale, or to turn various shades of purple or red. Magnesium deficiencies are usually remedied by spraying the leaves.

Calcium is usually deficient in very wet, acid soils. Affected plants die back at growing points, stems and stalks wilt and no tubers are produced.

Sulphur deficiency retards a plant's growth because sulphur occupies a vital place in the formation of certain protein molecules. This is not a problem in regions, such as Britain, where sulphurous gases continually enter the atmosphere from industrial and domestic chimneys.

B. Minerals known as trace elements, which are required in minute quantities.

Iron, like magnesium, is an essential constituent of chlorophyll, and its absence causes light green or yellow leaf formation. In England, iron deficiencies are most notable on calcareous soils, e.g. on the chalk of the Downs and the Chilterns. Nowadays iron deficiencies are rectified by adding *cholates* to the soils: these are special organic compounds which enable iron ions to pass directly into plants.

Manganese aids a plant's respiration and encourages the synthesis of protein. In England calcareous soils tend to be deficient in this mineral.

Boron is essential to all plants: its absence causes deformities, especially in root crops.

Copper is required by plants in extremely small quantities, e.g. for proper growth the dry matter in the leaves of apple trees should contain 3·5 parts *per million* by weight of the metal. In places on the South Downs copper deficiencies formerly prevented the growth of cereal crops, and caused sheep to produce abnormal wool. The deficiencies can be rectified by spraying a weak (0·1 per cent) solution of copper sulphate, or by placing small pieces of copper metal in the drinking troughs of animals.

Zinc and *molybdenum* are also needed by plants in exceedingly minute quantities (about 10–40:1 million and 1:1 million parts by weight, respectively).

---

[1] Sir E. John Russell, op. cit., p. 183.

tion in their crumb structure. Soils affected in this way become unusually dusty and dry during a drought, and abnormally compact and water-logged when it rains. Waterlogging reduces the number of air spaces in the topsoil and cuts down the population of vital aerobic bacteria: the result is a decline in fertility. Thus a soil cannot be kept 'in good heart' simply by adding inorganic fertilizers. Organic wastes must also be supplied so that sufficient *humus* is evolved in the soil: it is this dark-brown, spongy, complex substance which keeps soil particles in a workable condition. At present manures are largely wasted outside north-west Europe and eastern Monsoon Asia. This is due to a variety of reasons, including ignorance of their beneficial properties, shortage of fuel, lack of labour and transport facilities, and, in the case of human excreta, the possibility of spreading disease. The almost world-wide failure to return human excreta to the land involves a tragic waste of valuable plant nutrients. Millions of tonnes of sewage are discharged daily into rivers, lakes and seas, where as well as being wasted it gives rise to serious problems of pollution. Pilot schemes for converting sewage into sterilized fertilizer sludge for farmers have proved feasible, but relatively expensive. In the U.S.A. some promising experiments have been conducted into the use of processed sewage as a food in which to grow algae, the algae in turn providing protein-rich fodder for livestock and food for human consumption.

Much fuller use could also be made of chemical fertilizers, especially on pasture land. In Britain, for example, only about one-half of the pastures ever receives a dressing of fertilizer, even though its application would almost certainly lead to an increase in the output of livestock products by 50–200 per cent. One major difficulty in the use of chemical fertilizers in an arid region, or one in which the rainfall or irrigation water supply is sporadic, is that the chemicals are liable to burn and damage growing plants unless they are washed into the soil soon after being spread. Much more can also be done to increase crop yields by improving crop rotations. It is most important in this respect to introduce legumes (e.g. lucerne, clover, peas and beans), for the bacteria which live in nodules on the roots of these plants are able to 'fix' atmospheric nitrogen into the soil. By enriching the soil in this way it is possible to diversify and improve crop

Bricks being made from animal dung in an Indian village.

production. Experiments in Greece and other Mediterranean countries show that yields of wheat and other cereals can be doubled by including legumes as an annual crop, planted after the cereal harvest. As yet the use of regular crop rotations is largely absent over much of south and east Asia, Africa and Latin America.

9. Plant and animal breeding

Plant and animal breeding on a scientific basis dates back to the 18th century, but the full impact of biological research on world agriculture has only begun to be felt during recent decades. One of the most promising discoveries has been *hybridization*, i.e. the creation of plants with new genetic combinations. This makes it possible to evolve new species of plants with greatly improved yields. In the U.S.A., for example, the increasing use of hybrids is one of the main reasons why total food production has more than doubled during the past thirty years, despite the fact that the total cultivated area has diminished by 13 per cent. Spectacular increases have resulted from the use of hybrid cereals. In the mid-1930s the U.S. maize output, using non-hybrid seed, averaged 53 million tonnes per annum, with an average yield of 1·5 tonnes per hectare: today over 80 per cent of the maize seed consists of hybrids and the total annual output is about 115 million tonnes, with an average yield of 3·3 tonnes per hectare. Other famous examples of cereal hybrids in North America include Red Fife and Marquis wheats, the latter being developed in western Canada by crossing European and indigenous Indian varieties of the plant. Much research on hybrids is also being done in Europe, notably by Italian experts working under Shell Italiana at Borgo a Mozzano in Tuscany. Similar work in Britain has produced special strains of quick-growing grasses, e.g. one Italian ryegrass used on the Reading University Farm cropped three times in May. By sowing hybrid grasses which anticipate the spring, farmers can harvest several hay crops each year, which enables them to increase the number of their livestock.

As yet the planting of hybrid seed is largely confined to economically advanced countries, but efforts are being made, mainly under the auspices of the Food and Agriculture Organization of the United Nations, to spread its use in underdeveloped territories. General use of hybrid and selected seeds, accompanied by appropriate

Experimental plots at Rothamsted Experimental Station, Herts.

dressings of fertilizer, would almost certainly raise cereal crop yields by up to 200 per cent. In the U.S.A., for example, wheat yields are about 1·7 tonnes/hectare, compared with yields of 0·75–1·0 tonnes/hectare over most of Asia, Latin America and Africa. Similarly U.S. yields of sorghum are about 2·5 tonnes/hectare as compared with about 0·5 tonnes/hectare over most of Asia and Africa. Failure to use good-quality seed is partly attributable to the fact that many farmers do not know of its existence, but also to its higher cost and heavier fertilizer requirements as compared with normal varieties. Of the rice-growing countries of Monsoon Asia only Japan has made a systematic effort over a long period to improve the varieties grown by farmers, as a result of which more than 70 per cent of the Japanese rice fields are today sown with high-quality seed. Attempts are also being made in various parts of south and east Asia to cross the *indica* and *japonica* types of rice, with the aim of combining the adaptability of the former to humid sub-tropical conditions with the responsiveness to fertilizers and high potential yields of the latter. As rice is the staple food of some 1700 million people any advance towards improving rice yields is clearly of the utmost importance.

Another promising line of botanical research involves the use of synthetic hormones to regulate the growth rate and size of plants. Many of these hormones are extraordinarily potent, a pinch or two being sufficient for a hectare of crops to grow faster and larger. In fact the use of hormones promises radically to alter the whole concept of plant geography, for they make it possible to extend, contract or shift the growing season of a crop, to ripen it at a desired moment, and partially to offset the normal effects upon it of such hazards as drought, cold and disease. All this can be done by administering synthetic hormones because they trigger off the intricate chemical reactions within a growing plant whereby it utilizes its food and regulates its life cycle. Hitherto the use of synthetic hormones has been restricted, partly because of their high cost but also because in many cases insufficient time has yet elapsed to test the possible ill effects of their application. It seems likely, however, that eventually they will have as dramatic an impact in raising plant yields as the use of fertilizers and insecticides. One of the most amazing hormones is *gibberellin*, which repays handsomely for being sprayed on most crops, in spite of its high retail price of about £3 per gramme. An outstanding example is the Thompson seedless grape, some vines of which were sprayed with gibberellin in California.

The treated grapes were so much plumper and juicier that they sold for $8.80 per twenty-five-pound lug on the New York produce market, while untreated Thompsons went for $5.78. A two-phase treatment works best with grapes. First, the vineyard is sprayed with a dosage of four to six grams per acre shortly after the flowers come into full bloom; this increases the fruit 'set' and ensures uniform bunches. Later, another eight to sixteen grams per acre makes the grapes grow; they get 25 to 50 per cent larger than normal, and the juice content increases. Gibberellin also increases the length of the peduncles, the stemlets attached to the individual fruits. This opens up the bunches, making them less vulnerable to rot. Finally, gibberellin adds a bonus to its aid to grape growers: it makes it unnecessary to girdle the vines—i.e. remove a ring of bark from the stem to keep nutrients from flowing back into the roots. Girdling is at best an expensive hand process, and it is apt to damage very young and very old vines.

Gibberellin has been tried on many kinds of citrus fruits, with happy results. It increases the fruit set as well as adding to the pulp content and thinning the rind. Seed potatoes are more productive if they are dipped in gibberellin solution before planting. Ordinarily only two or three of the forty-five eyes on a potato will sprout, but a dose of gibberellin makes more than half of them sprout. Gibberellin also makes barley sprout rapidly and uniformly, an effect gratifying to the brewers, who make their malt from sprouted barley. . . . The economics of gibberellin are less favourable for crops that are already cheaply produced. It may be worth while to spray wheat, for the chemical appears to ripen the crop two weeks ahead of schedule, thus reducing the danger of rust. In cold climates, where one hay crop per season is the rule, gibberellin might make two crops possible by forcing the grass into growing earlier in the spring and keeping it growing later in the fall. Dozens of other applications of gibberellin have been tried, but vast areas of potential use remain to be explored. It may, for example, prove to be an effective weapon against some forms of plant virus disease. Preliminary tests show that it does not get rid of the virus, but it gives a plant the strength to survive despite its disease. Gibberellin-treated asters, corn, and crimson clover have grown to normal size despite infection with stunting viruses. And, in one experiment, diseased strawberries produced runners that were free of virus because the plants actually grew faster than the virus could spread.[1]

Other synthetic hormones have an effect exactly opposite to that of gibberellin, i.e. they act as a plant tranquillizer and produce healthy dwarfs: with certain plants this has advantages in market gardening.

Hormones can also be injected into animals, to alter and control their growth and reproduction rates, and to alter the proportion of such items as fat, lean meat, bone and hair in their body make-up. Animals are particularly influenced by the amount and periodicity of sunlight. For example, electric light can be used to simulate daylight and so induce laying fowls to increase their output of eggs. Attempts have also been made to induce double breeding in sheep and cattle by artificially lengthening the hours of light to anticipate the coming of spring. Another whole new field in animal breeding has been opened up by using the technique of artificial insemination. This process, developed in Denmark in the 1930s, makes it possible to fertilize thousands of cows from one particularly fine bull, even though the bull may be living in another continent. In Denmark a prize bull called Horsen Høg made 6300 cows pregnant in a single year. By the 1960s over one-half of the entire stock of dairy cattle in Great Britain had been bred artificially, a trend accompanied by a big increase in the average output of milk per cow (2870 litres per cow in 1948; 3685 litres per cow in 1968). Not all of this increase is attributable to the use of artificial insemination, however, for big efforts have also been made to eradicate disease, especially tuberculosis, mastitis and contagious abortion. With modern deep-freezing devices it is possible that artificial insemination will have even more profound effects, for semen can now be stockpiled for use with future generations of animals. Yet another technique for improving the quality of livestock is to transfer the ovum of a prize cow to another one, called the 'incubator',

[1] George A. W. Boehm, *Farming With Hormones*, Readings in Economic Geography, ed. Ward and Hoffman, Holt, Rinehart & Winston, New York.

and then fertilize it with semen from a quality bull. As a cow in her lifetime produces some 1700 ova it is possible to build up a herd of pedigree beef or dairy cattle from a single pair of beasts within a relatively short space of time. It seems likely, too, that the use of 'fertility drugs' will eventually make it possible to decide in advance both the number and the sex of the progeny of an animal at each conception.

The successful breeding of high-quality animals has so far been limited largely to the temperate regions. In the tropics, especially in Africa, ownership of livestock tends to be regarded more as a status symbol than as a source of profit and consequently there is a greater interest in numbers than in nutrition.

On a European farm beef cattle are slaughtered at the age of 18 months to 3 years, giving a rapid turnover and good returns on capital, whereas amongst some pastoralist tribes cattle are sold only when cash is urgently required for some specific purpose and slaughter is delayed until the death of a beast appears imminent. The difference can be attributed in part to the fact that on a ranch run commercially livestock are raised primarily as a means of making money for purchasing other goods, whereas amongst pastoralists owning animals is an end in itself as much as a means to an end. Like the ownership of a car by a town-dweller, it promotes a feeling of pride and a status that could not easily be acquired otherwise. The family herds have often been compared to a bank balance that can be drawn upon when unusual demands are made on the family finances. Such demands are greatest when marriage by one of the male members is in view and the young men who perform the hard and tedious work of tending the animals are anxious to see their flocks and herds grow in size, so that they may have wives themselves and rear children who will enable them, as soon as possible, to lead the more leisured existence of their fathers. Furthermore, people like the Fulani depend on milk for their food, and since lactation depends on calves, the main interest of the herd owner is in a steady yearly increase in his herds.

In the past when losses by disease were greater and political conditions less favourable, numbers in herds probably fluctuated violently. In recent years numbers of cattle have been increasing and many rangelands show signs of being overgrazed, with deteriorating pastures and eroding soils.[1]

The new African governments, however, are anxious to increase the meat protein in their peoples' diets, and to prevent overstocking. This is slowly being achieved by persuading herd owners to slaughter a large proportion of their stock once a year for sale. This introduces the profit motive and stimulates a desire to own better-quality beasts. At present most tropical cattle are small, scraggy and inferior cross-breeds. In Africa, for example, they mostly consist of mixtures of Zebu, Dwarf Shorthorn and Hamitic Longhorn. Some of these native animals are unusually resistant to disease and they have been used in selective breeding experiments to produce higher-quality beasts such as the Santa Gertrudis of Texas, the Sindhi and Sahiwal cattle of India and the African Boron. In Africa selective breeding has been shown to treble milk yields and double meat production.[2]

It is sometimes argued that animal husbandry is too wasteful, and that a world faced with an endemic food crisis should concentrate entirely on cultivation. Where animals are fed with plant crops which could be eaten directly by man this argument has considerable weight, for there is an inevitable loss in energy at each stage of a food chain. (*Compare with fish food chains, p.* 118). One obvious case of a wasteful practice is the feeding of edible grains to broiler chickens. However, animals do not necessarily compete with men for food. The herbivores, in particular, can digest fibres such as cellulose, and other complex carbohydrates which man's digestive tract is unable to absorb. Ruminants such as cattle and sheep convert these fibres into meat and milk, so adding to the store of human foodstuffs. Unlike man, furthermore, herbivorous animals are able to derive amino acids from bacteriological proteins, and these valuable acids then become available in an edible form which men can digest. Animals also manufacture nutrients from the leaves and stems of fodder plants which are of little value to man. Another argument for retaining cattle is that they can convert into edible products various wastes, e.g. oilseed meals, sugar-beet and sugar-cane tops, chaff and other grain residues—all of which would otherwise be lost as human food.

[1] A. T. Grove, *Africa South of the Sahara*, O.U.P., p. 56.

[2] A. T. Grove, op. cit.

Experiments suggest that advanced societies generate a big increase in demand for meat, especially beef, and that in the Western world there are no readily acceptable alternatives to meat and milk. (*See, however, p. 111 as regards the use of substitute milk in Monsoon Asia.*) To supply new types of meat, experiments are in progress in South Africa and in the Soviet Union to test the possibility of domesticating wild animals such as antelope and deer. Meanwhile rapid progress is being made in the 'improvement' of old domesticated species such as cattle, pigs and poultry. The object is to produce animals and birds which mature faster on a smaller food intake, i.e. to make them more efficient converters of fodder into edible food products. At the same time modern research aims to produce animals which can utilize industrial 'wastes' such as cellulose and molasses.

10. Control of pests and diseases

Pests and diseases make tremendous inroads on food production, even in economically advanced countries where farmers can afford to enlist the aid of chemical pesticides, fungicides and weedkillers. Damage to crops and animals can be caused by an enormous variety of enemies, including fungi, viruses, bacteria, insects, mites, rabbits, birds and weeds. In addition standing crops and pastures can be trampled underfoot and eaten, and livestock attacked or scattered, by wandering groups of wild animals such as elephants, deer, prairie dogs and even kangaroos. Notable past disasters include the notorious potato blight which caused the great Irish famine of the mid-19th century; the virtual destruction in the 1870s of Ceylon's coffee export trade following the spread of a fungus (*Hemileia vastatrix*) which destroyed the coffee plants' leaves; and the havoc caused to French vineyards in the 1880s by a plant-louse (*Phylloxera*): wine production in 1880–90 was reduced by two-fifths compared with the previous decade. Generally

(Top) *Emaciated cross-bred cattle on the Nigerian Savanna.*

(Centre) *Prime herd of pedigree Friesians in Somerset.*

(Bottom) *Brahman cow with calf at an agricultural show in Jamaica.*

speaking the problem of pests and diseases has worsened as farming has become more intensive and specialized. The modern tendency is to create large concentrations of particular crops and animals, sometimes under 'hot-house' or 'fact-ory-farming' conditions which make the environment even more favourable for parasites. One illustration of this problem is the widespread appearance of rusts in barley and other cereal crops on the recently cultivated chalklands of southern England, the spores apparently being blown from field to field and from one area to the next. Another difficulty is the emergence of disease-resistant strains of viruses and bacteria which are immune to normal sprays and injections. The magnitude of the overall problem can be judged from the following estimates[1] of food losses which accrue to farmers in the U.S.A. *every year*:

5000 million dollars worth of potential food destroyed by weeds
4000 million dollars worth of potential food destroyed by insects
4000 million dollars worth of potential food destroyed by disease
2000 million dollars worth of potential food destroyed by rats

The grand total of 15 000 million dollars amounts to the staggering proportion of 40 per cent of

> ... the potential saleable portion of (each) farmer's crop each year.[2]

In recent years new organic chemical pesticides have become available, which, if their use became general, could almost certainly increase total farm outputs in North America, Western Europe and the Soviet Union by one-third during the next half century. On certain major crops the increase in yields would probably be one-half or more, and in less developed parts of the world the results would be even more spectacular. The quantities of chemicals needed to give protection are remarkably small but extremely effective. For example a single kilogramme of 'carbamate' can protect enough wheat seed for 140 hectares; four days aircraft spraying of 'dieldrin' has been known to save over 140 000 hectares of Californian rice from a rare leaf-eating bug; and

wireworm infestation can now be cured as effectively with one gramme of 'lindane' as with ten kilogrammes of naphthalene, the commonest preventative which has so far been used. Some of the new chemicals are relatively cheap. In the U.S.A., for example,

> It now costs one-half as much as formerly to control rangeland and cropland pests like grasshoppers, and the control efficiency has risen from 60 per cent to 98 per cent. . . . The control of greenbugs with the new insecticides has increased wheat yields in Oklahoma by as much as 400 per cent; alfalfa-seed production in Utah has risen 150 per cent; hybrid-corn production increases due to better insect control are estimated at 30 per cent; Maine potato production can be increased 100 per cent. . . . The chemical control of livestock pests is now saving the nation as a whole some $800 million a year.[3]

The use of chemicals also greatly reduces the amount of labour needed on the land, for hand-weeding is virtually eliminated.

One of the most potent groups of organic compounds comprises the insecticides, and it is against insects that farmers at present direct their main attack—even though weeds cause greater damage. Most of the new insecticides are neurotoxins, i.e. they paralyse and kill an insect by attacking its central nervous system. The most famous neurotoxin is DDT (*di*chloro*di*phenyl*tri*-chloroethane), which combines a high killing power with a long residual effect. DDT is extremely effective in dealing with insects as varied as potato beetles, houseflies and mosquitoes, but in the long run resistant strains of insects are thrown up by genetical mutation. These require a much stronger killing dose and so there is a constant search for new and more effective neurotoxins. Details of some of these are given at the top of the opposite page.

One of the most effective campaigns being waged with the aid of neurotoxic insecticides is that against the hordes of desert locusts which from time immemorial have plagued parts of south-west Asia and North Africa. Since 1960 twenty governments have participated in an all-out onslaught to control and prevent the ravages of this voracious grasshopper. In the Middle East the F.A.O. co-ordinates the attack, focal points of which are the insects' breeding grounds

1 Eric Hodgins, *Farming's Chemical Age*, Fortune, p. 23.
2 The American Chemical Society.
3 Eric Hodgins, op. cit.

located within the Arabian peninsula. Locust eggs are laid a few centimetres below the surface of desert sand and the most vulnerable phase of the insect's life is immediately after it has been hatched, for at that time it cannot fly. Once the location of a breeding ground has been pinpointed, tens of millions of young locusts can be destroyed by timely spraying of the ground with insecticides. The photograph shows the effect of spraying aldrin on a locust swarm in Pakistan. One swarm destroyed by aircraft in northern Somalia in 1960 was estimated to weigh 30 000 tonnes. Results in Arabia have been so good that major locust plagues are now a rarity in the Old World and it is hoped that eventually this dreaded pest will be eliminated. Similar methods have already brought victory over the locust *Schistocerca paranensis* Burm., which until the 1950s devastated a multitude of crops in Mexico and Central America. According to F.A.O. estimates the application of modern anti-locust methods in all the world's affected regions would increase the total world output of food and animal fodder crops by some 15 per cent, at a cost amounting to only a tiny portion of the value of the additional output.

Although DDT-type pesticides are extremely effective their use has recently been severely restricted in N. America, Sweden, Denmark and the U.K. This is because research shows that the environment has in places become dangerously contaminated with DDT residues. In certain fish and birds (e.g. the peregrine falcon and golden eagle) such residues have accumulated in sufficient quantities to cause reproductive failures and some deaths. Although there is no definite evidence that the amount of DDT residue at present consumed in human foods is harmful, it is feared that ill-effects might result if their intake is augmented. There is also evidence that when DDT kills micro-organisms in the soil it adversely upsets the delicate balance in it and reduces its fertility. The continued use of neuro-toxin insecticides must therefore be weighed against the facts of increasingly widespread wild-life poisoning, crop pollution and damage to the soil.

Herbicides (weedkillers) promise to be even more helpful in the long run than insecticides, for weeds are responsible for greater farm losses than any other single cause. This is mainly because weeds are exceedingly widespread and compete for plant nutrients, water and light during the early and vulnerable stages of a crop's growth. The average ragweed, for example, needs three times as much water as does a maize plant. Similarly one common mustard plant needs four times as much water, four times as much potash and twice as much phosphorus and nitro-

Red Locust (Nomadacris Septemfasciata).

gen as a well-established oat plant. Experiments in the U.S.A. have shown that the application of chemical weedkillers can increase the yield of maize in an average season *seven*fold. As yet, however, only about one-tenth of the cropland of the U.S.A. receives weedkiller treatment. The most effective herbicides belong to the phenoxy group of chemicals (2,4-dichlorophenoxyacetic acid, or '2,4-D'), which kill weeds by stimulating their growth to such an extent that they 'burn themselves out'. They are also selective, in that they kill broadleaved plants but leave grasses alone. This makes them particularly advantageous for use with cereals after the corn is up, a

few kilogrammes of 2,4-D per hectare being sufficient to destroy most weeds without disturbing the growing corn. 2,4-D has proved an invaluable boon to wheat farmers on the Canadian prairies, where weeds are the principal pests. As phenoxy herbicides are not poisonous they are also very useful on grass fodder crops, bringing certain death to such noxious pests as bull thistle, giant ragweed and cocklebur. Phenoxy compounds can also be sprayed over a newly planted field to kill young weed seedlings as their shoots appear: the seeds of the wanted crop are not affected because of their depth of planting and their herbicide tolerance. Yet another phenoxy preparation kills scrub and woody plants but is harmless to grasses and wildlife, which makes it possible to eradicate mesquite and sagebrush growing on arid pasture lands by spraying chemicals from an aircraft. The Colorado Experiment Station reckons that about 1·6 of the 2·8 million hectares of sagebrush land in Colorado could be cleared in this way, and that the treated land would increase its output of livestock products by more than threefold. Large-scale reclamation projects are also feasible in the 30 million hectares of mesquite-infested land in Texas and New Mexico, and in similar semi-arid grazing lands in other countries. Chemicals such as 2,4-D can also be used as growth regulators on specific crops—the job for which they were

A locust swarm in the Sudan.

originally intended. Details are given in the table below. At present, mainly because of the high cost, these practices are mainly experimental, but it seems likely that in time they will be employed commercially.

Fungicides are making a big impact on the yields of fruit orchards, greenhouses and market gardens. They are an enormous boon in the farmers' fight against such fungal diseases as apple scab, late blight on potatoes and the stem rust of wheat. A remarkable instance of the effectiveness of the new chemical fungicides—most of which are carbamates—has been the virtual elimination of grape mildew in the vineyards of Afghanistan. Until 1958 this disease, which causes grapes to disintegrate and emit an offensive odour, caused an average loss of 50 per cent of the grape crop in the vineyards around Kohdaman and 80 per cent of those in

The effect of spraying the soil insecticide Dieldrin on a Herts. field. The unsprayed, left portion, of the field, shows feeble crop growth.

SOME WAYS IN WHICH CHEMICAL GROWTH REGULATORS CAN BE EMPLOYED

To thin out the blossoms on fruit trees and thus produce a better set of fruit;
To delay fruit budding until the danger of frosts is past;
To prevent fruit from dropping;
To produce fruits without seeds;
To halt flowering where not wanted, as with vegetables like spinach and broccoli;
To alter the shape of plants for easier harvesting;
To prevent sprouting in stored potatoes or grains;
To slow the growth of grass and thus reduce the number of mowings;
To stimulate root formation, as for the rooting of cuttings;
To accelerate ripening, and thus permit growers of heavy produce like pineapples to stagger ripening to fit canning schedules.[1]

---

[1] Eric Hodgins, op. cit., p. 28.

Kataghan and Chardeh Ghorband. Losses amounted to some £15 million annually. Following spraying demonstrations by an F.A.O. expert the disease has all but been eradicated, its incidence falling to less than 3 per cent in vineyards which have taken preventative action. Fungicides are also being widely used to disinfect seeds prior to planting, so that they can ward off attack by micro-organisms in the soil. Disinfection is particularly desirable with hybrid cereal seeds, for these are relatively expensive, and farmers cannot risk their succumbing to fungus attack before sprouting.

Chemicals are also being used as defoliants, e.g. to bring about a rapid collapse of the leaves and stems of potato plants so that their tubers attain a higher quality. Defoliation also facilitates the

harvesting of legumes such as soya beans. Chemicals are also spread on the land as soil conditioners, to make a soil more friable. This is achieved by causing chemical reactions which change the crumb structure of the soil. A better crumb structure in turn makes the soil more stable under the effects of heavy rainfall, reduces its tendency to bake and crack in hot sunshine, and increases its ability to absorb and retain moisture. Soil conditioning is particularly effective on heavy, stiff clays such as Weald Clay and Oxford Clay, which suffer from bad drainage and a lack of soil atmosphere. Chemical conditioning can lead to increases in the yield of root crops by 50–100 per cent.

The many advantages of using farm chemicals have been emphasized above, but there are also serious liabilities. Traces of pesticides are now found in virtually all animals and man, and there is the risk that the amounts may reach dangerous proportions. Reference has been made above to birds of prey succumbing to fatal amounts of toxic chemicals obtained through food chains. Hundreds of new agricultural chemicals come on to the market each year and although they are tested for direct health hazards their long-term effects on biological processes are largely unknown. Chemical sprays also bring about the unintended killing of bees and butterflies and so endanger pollination. Great increases in the yields of crops resulting from the use of chemicals can also bring about gluts, with attendant economic and political troubles. Furthermore the use of chemicals often permits a drastic reduction in the demand for farm labour, and so can spark off unemployment problems.

A good example of the effects of pest destruction on farm output is seen in New Zealand, where rabbits have caused millions of pounds worth of damage since they were first introduced in 1838. By the 1870s their numbers were giving rise to serious concern, especially in the Otago, Marlborough and Canterbury districts of South Island. The native tussock grasslands had been burnt off and grazed by sheep, producing sparsely covered, dry, friable soils ideal for rabbit warrens. Rabbits soon became a plague, devouring all available grasses, and many sheep-farmers were ruined. Large numbers of rabbits were killed by poisoning and trapping, but although a thriving export trade developed in rabbit skins and carcases, it made good only a fraction of the losses resulting from damaged sheep pastures. The heaviest infestations of rabbits were in areas of low rainfall and friable, well-drained soils, where their ubiquitous burrowing and grazing were a contributory cause of soil erosion and an obstacle to schemes for re-grassing. Campaigns to exterminate the rabbits made little headway while trappers could make a profit, for some animals were always spared by the hunters to keep themselves in business. Thus in 1947 a Rabbit Nuisance Amendment Act introduced a levy on exported rabbit skins, and in 1954 the export of rabbit carcases was prohibited. A Rabbit Destruction Council was also established by the Government to supervise and make grants to local Rabbit Boards throughout the country. The total cost to the New Zealand anti-rabbit campaign now runs at more than £1 million per annum. Results of the new 'killer policy' have been impressive. For example, the areas within Rabbit Districts classed as 'heavily infested' dropped from 1 715 000 hectares in 1948 to 121 500 hectares in 1969, and during the same period the number of skins exported fell from 13 471 298 to nil.[1] The benefits of sheepfarming are not so easily measured but many farms cleared of rabbits are carrying more sheep and shearing more wool per sheep. On ploughable land, cultivation and reseeding can quickly restore pastures once the rabbits have gone, but on steep country natural recovery may take some time. Here, farmers are wisely refraining from increasing the size of their flocks, but are already enjoying heavier wool-clips and improved lambing rates. A recent survey of Central Otago speaks of

> a new cycle of plant cover from spring onwards —the 'green tinge', where before no species could survive the close grazing of the rabbits. . . . Real security for New Zealand's farmlands will come only with the complete eradication of the rabbit pest, and the Council is aiming at nothing less.[2]

One loophole is that there are still a few infested areas where farmers cater for the local market in rabbit meat. Efforts are being made to have all such areas brought under board control and to suppress the carcase trade within New Zealand itself.

Disease control in domesticated animals is also bringing in dividends in the form of increased yields of meat, milk, hides, skins and eggs. Veterinary measures such as vaccination and the quarantine and/or slaughter of infected herds have become universal in the more advanced countries and are increasingly being adopted in underdeveloped territories (*See also notes on page 40*). An interesting and possibly far-reaching example of the impact of modern veterinary techniques on a developing economy can be seen in Uganda, where the present Five-Year Plan emphasizes the vital necessity of expanding the livestock industry. One major problem is the

[1] Section 121 of the Agricultural Pests Destruction Act 1967 states: "No person shall (a) sell or offer for sale; or (b) export from New Zealand for sale any rabbit skins or rabbit carcase produced in New Zealand."

[2] J S. Duncan, 'Combating the Rabbit Pest in New Zealand', *Geography* No. 196, p. 122.

92

control of insect-borne diseases such as try-panosomiasis or 'nagana', a disease caused by a parasite which is carried from one animal to another by the blood-sucking tsetse fly. The map shows the extent to which the distribution of cattle in Uganda is affected by tsetse infestation. It is possible to keep cattle in areas with light medium density of tsetse by the use of expensive drugs, but this method is often uneconomic. Hence the expansion of the livestock industry mainly hinges on the eradication of tsetse.

Since 1955 this has in fact been achieved in the south-east Bunyoro area of Western Uganda, with the result that livestock farming has developed on an unprecedented scale. Cattle trypanosomiasis is spread in East Africa by two species of tsetse fly, both of which thrive in well-wooded Savana vegetation where they can obtain shade and a ready food supply from the blood of game or cattle. Between 1951 and 1955 all wild game such as buffalo and bush pig were systematically cleared from south-east Bunyoro in order to eliminate the food supply of the fly. At the same time a 5 kilometre wide zone around the tsetse-freed area was cleared for intensive cultivation to form a 'consolidation barrier' against reincursion of the fly from infested areas (*see map*). It was reckoned that flies could not cross this barrier because it contained no game or cattle on which they could feed and no shady bush vegetation. 3000 Zebu cattle were then brought in from east Uganda to initiate the Bunyoro Ranching Scheme. At first the Scheme was threatened by considerable tsetse re-incursion but this has now been remedied, mainly by using insecticide sprays within the consolidation barrier, clearing more bush and hunting game which had re-entered the cleared land. The main problem now is to encourage settlers to make permanent homes in this barrier zone, for otherwise the re-growth of bush there will destroy the protection from tsetse which it affords the Bunyoro Ranch.

On the Ranch there are now well over 10 000 cattle. Although the animals are free from 'nagana' there are many other diseases from which they have to be protected by frequent spraying and vaccination, including tick-borne infections, anthrax, brucellosis, blackquarter, haemorrhagic septicaemia and fascioliasis.

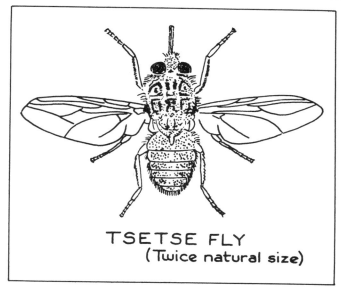

TSETSE FLY
(Twice natural size)

Outside the ranch there is also increased awareness of the importance of tick-borne diseases and twice-weekly spraying against ticks is required by law on all dairy farms with imported cattle such as Jerseys and Friesians. The Government makes strict requirements for tick-free enclosed pastures before such grade cattle can be introduced, and there is a Government Livestock Subsidy Scheme enabling farmers to purchase wire and fencing posts at a reduced price.[1]

Vigorous efforts are also being made to improve animal welfare by (i) increasing the number of waterholes and water storage tanks, (ii) improving the quality of fodder grasses, (iii) keeping a strict check on secondary growth of bush by

[1] Brenda J. Turner and P. Randall Baker, 'Tsetse Control and Livestock Development, A Case Study from Uganda', *Geography*, No. 240, p. 249.

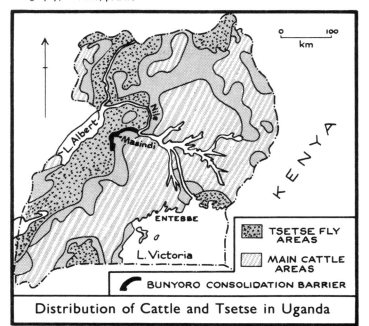

Distribution of Cattle and Tsetse in Uganda

repeated cutting and the use of arboricides and (iv) organizing rotation grazing, if possible in fenced, weed-free paddocks. These improvements in disease control and in management are now enabling non-indigenous cattle to be brought into the area.

Boran bulls were imported from Kenya in 1964 to replace small Zebu bulls lacking in size and beef qualities. By the end of 1966 there were 42 Boran Bulls on the Bunyoro Ranching Scheme and a total of approximately 1000 relatively high-grade Borans and about 2000 Boran-Zebu crosses. The Bunyoro Growers Co-operative Ranch, begun in 1966, had 200 Kenya Borans among the 380 head of cattle at the end of that year. In the annual livestock returns, January 1967, it was also recorded that 18 dairy farms had exotic cattle, the most popular being Jersey, Friesian and Guernsey respectively. Half of these farms had under 20 hectares of fenced land and under 10 cows, and 15 out of 18 farms had under 20 dairy cows, so as yet dairy farming is only on a small scale, though intensive. Some measure of the present rate of expansion comes from the Bunyoro Growers Co-operative Union Dairy in Masindi. This dairy was established in August 1966; after 6 months 17 people were delivering milk to the dairy and after 12 months 42 people were enrolled. Apart from local contracts with the hospital and secondary school, for example, 318 litres are now sent every alternate day by van to Kampala (217 kilometres) and there is no doubt that all the output will be readily absorbed by the expanding domestic market. ... South-east Bunyoro shows the advantage of tsetse eradication in enabling livestock development. It also shows that, by the development of the water resources and improved management and breeding, the productivity of the area can be increased both to the advantage of the local economy and to the aid of the developing ranches in other areas.[1]

These developments in Uganda, especially the introduction of high-yielding, exotic dairy cattle, are of great interest, for the table (*above*) shows that at present most tropical lands are characterized by a very low productivity of their milk cattle. This is particularly serious because the efficiency of conversion of animal feed to human food is greater in the case of the milk cow than for any other animal, except for the pig. It seems

[1] Brenda J. Turner and P. Randall Baker, op. cit.

likely that the modern methods of disease control used at Bunyoro will in time spread to other tropical grasslands in Africa and elsewhere, with resulting improvements both in land use and in the diet and health of the inhabitants.

MILK PRODUCTION IN CERTAIN COUNTRIES kg/milking cow	
North-Central U.S.A.	4124
Jamaica	1746
Ecuador	1118
Brazil	644
India	189
India (approved farms)	1845
Malaya	376
Botswana	1674
Somalia	810
Malawi	119

Source: F.A.O.

11. Mechanization and equipment

Technical changes, involving the use of tractor- and animal-drawn implements, modern hand tools and more economic patterns of farm management, can play a vital role in improving farming yields. The improvements accrue partly from the use of more effective equipment, but also because mechanization makes it possible to carry out farming operations more quickly and at the precise time calculated to maximize outputs. In western Canada, for example, the increasing substitution of tractors for horses has greatly shortened the time farmers have to spend on the sowing of spring wheat. This enables them to cultivate their fallow land before it becomes infested with weeds in the early summer, a practice which was not feasible when horse-drawn equipment was used. The result is a substantial diminution of weeds, and increased cereal crop yields. More spectacular, and probably more far-reaching, is the impact of rice 'planting machines' in the Far East, where traditional methods entail the putting in of every single rice plant by hand at an immense cost in back-breaking toil. In China simple machines, constructed mostly of bamboo, wood and a few metal parts, have been in use since 1958. Depending on local conditions the machines do from 3 to 20 times the amount of work of a hand-planter, thus greatly shortening the time needed to plant a rice crop.

This is especially important for areas with two crops per season. It is considered essential that planting of the second crop should be completed by the Chinese 'beginning of Autumn' (August 7th). Any days in advance of this will increase the yield. A planting completed 12 days before this date is estimated to give double the yield of a planting completed two days after it. It is claimed that in Kweichow in 1960, using planters in some three-fifths of the province's paddy fields, there was a saving of 2 million working days. The regularity of depth and spacing obtained using planters is also claimed to be significant, and the speeding up of the operation of transfer from nursery bed to field at the right stage of growth all help to increase yields by 2 to 35 per cent in otherwise comparable conditions.[2]

The photograph shows a motor-driven rice-tiller which has been specially developed for use in small fields in Japan.

Some agronomists maintain that the most effective way in which the West can help farmers in underdeveloped lands to help themselves is by making available simple mechanical devices of this type.

A breakthrough seems at last to be on the way. The West has begun to realize that the purpose of aid should be to stimulate self-help. So far, aid programmes have tended to bypass the bulk of the people they were supposed to benefit. A large proportion of the money has gone into urban or industrial projects. Hydro-electric dams and heavy industrial plant are the most glaring examples. The West has been exporting something like its own technology, evolved to save labour, to societies which lack almost everything *except* labour and whose crying need is for labour-intensive projects.[3]

To this end a group of London businessmen recently produced a guide book, *Tools for Progress* for distribution throughout the developing world.

[2] W. J. Riding, 'Rice Revolution', *Geography*, No. 214, p. 96.

[3] Hugh Hanning, 'Of rice and men', *The Guardian*.

Among the tools illustrated are:

1. An animal-drawn tool-bar, supplied with about eight tools.
2. A mechanical rice-thresher for small-scale paddy growers.
3. A hand-operated groundnut decorticator.
4. A hand-operated coconut dehusker.
5. A rainwater catchment tank kit.
6. A hand-operated maize sheller.
7. A hydraulic ram pump.

The tools are not all agricultural. For the best incentive to raise production through new techniques is the availability of cheap consumer goods: footwear, bicycles, ceramics, furniture or whatever. Indeed, without such goods a rise in farm earnings can be counter-productive, as Freedom from Hunger once found to their cost in Kenya. There, the farmers had nothing on which to spend the new earnings gleaned from an otherwise admirable farm scheme—except alcohol. They took to the bottle with disastrous effects on morale. The group is in the business of encouraging the development of appropriate technologies and transferring information about them to developing countries.[1]

The need for improved tools and farm implements is almost universal throughout the under-developed territories. Over vast regions of the tropics, for example, cultivation by hand-hoe is the rule, and in some places not even hoes, but digging sticks are used to prepare the ground for cultivation. The photograph shows Latuko tribesmen from East Africa, breaking up the sun-dried soil of the Savana for planting millet. The Latuko have no knowledge of the plough and their long wooden paddles merely loosen the soil. It is arguable, however, that Western-style ploughing is not really suitable under conditions of heavy tropical rainfall, because of the dangers of soil erosion (*see also p. 32*). Some experts suggest that it is simpler, safer, and less likely to provoke rural under-employment, if subsistence farmers such as the Latuko are issued with steel-tipped hand-hoes, rather than mechanized ploughs. Where ploughs are already in use, however, and farming practices include soil conservation, big returns in improved farming efficiency and increased crop yields can be obtained by making available steel tips for wooden ploughshares, better-designed ploughs and, if the recipients are able to use them effectively, tractors to replace draught animals.

In fact the introduction of tractors can do more to transform traditional patterns of farming than any other technological change. Suitably fitted with tracks or special wheels, tractors make it possible to cultivate sloping and heavy land that would otherwise be mostly in permanent pasture or waste. Examples in Britain include the Keuper Marl in northern Northants, the blue Lias and London Clays of Essex and the Weald Clay of Surrey and Sussex. Only tractor-power makes it feasible to operate the enormous plough shown in the photograph on p. 70. This plough is carving a 5 metre furrow on a newly reclaimed Dutch polder. The substitution of tractors for horses or oxen had additional advantages in that it makes available for other uses a very large area of land that would otherwise be needed to provide fodder crops.

[1] Ibid.

Each horse needs 3 acres or more of land; each tractor releases at least twice that area of land for the growing of marketable food or fibre.[2]

Just how significant this is in terms of total food production can be judged from the fact that there are now well over 100 million tractors at work on the world's farms.

More modest technical improvements can also have an enormous effect. Such may be the replacement of head porterage by mule or donkey, the use of a proper harness in place of the clumsy yoking of oxen by their horns, the employment of the faster horse instead of the lumbering ox, or the provision of inflatable rubber tyres instead of the metal rims on wooden wheels common to many carts. Nor is it necessary to travel outside Europe to find areas where such innovations could be of great benefit. Early in the 1950s in the Italian commune of Borgo a Mozzano, remote in the mountains between Florence and Lucca, 95 per cent of goods were moved by human porterage and pack mules. Universally in the poorer parts of southern Europe, oxen yoked by the horns draw clumsy, solid-wheeled carts. In contrast to those modest improvements, the application of aerial methods to many agricultural operations catches the imagination. Since the last world war there has been a spectacular increase in such activities, including spraying, dressing, seeding, dropping rabbit poison in New Zealand and facilitating fence construction in otherwise inaccessible areas. In the short span of six years, the area

[2] A. N. Duckham, 'The Current Agricultural Revolution', *Geography*, No. 204.

treated by aerial means in the United States rose from almost 16 million hectares in 1951 almost 25 million in 1957 (*and to about 30 million in 1969[3]*). Such has been the growth of this technique that there is now a European Agricultural Aviation Centre at The Hague, issuing a quarterly journal. Undoubtedly aerial techniques are going to be of growing importance to farmers all over the world. Apart from improvements to the means of transport within the farm, it is important to notice also the development of devices for transport saving. This is closely related to the matter of work study. . . . An example is the design of yards so that cattle can feed from silage without the latter having to be cut and carted, or self-feeding, as it is called. Another method is the use of mobile milking units which can be placed in the fields, reducing the amount of walking required of the cattle.[4]

Improvements in rural transport facilities are particularly advantageous because of the economies in farm labour and storage costs which they make possible. These savings in turn help to make it economic for farmers to buy fertilizers and better equipment. Better transport also makes it possible for farmers to put their less accessible land to more productive use. In southern

[3] Aircraft in Agriculture. Federal Aviation Agency. Washington D. C.
[4] Michael Chisholm, *Rural Settlement and Land Use*, Hutchinson University Library, p. 173.

Primitive wooden plough on rough ground in the Lebanon.

England, for example, large tracts of former chalk downland have been brought under cultivation in recent decades. The map overleaf shows this trend on a single farm in Bignor, Sussex. Notice the position of the farm buildings in relation to the newly cultivated ground: before tractors replaced horses on this farm in 1935 it took half a day for a ploughing team to journey to and from the summit of the South Downs—today a tractor does the return trip in

Primitive device for husking coconuts in the West Indies.

Primitive scales used for weighing rice in Goa.

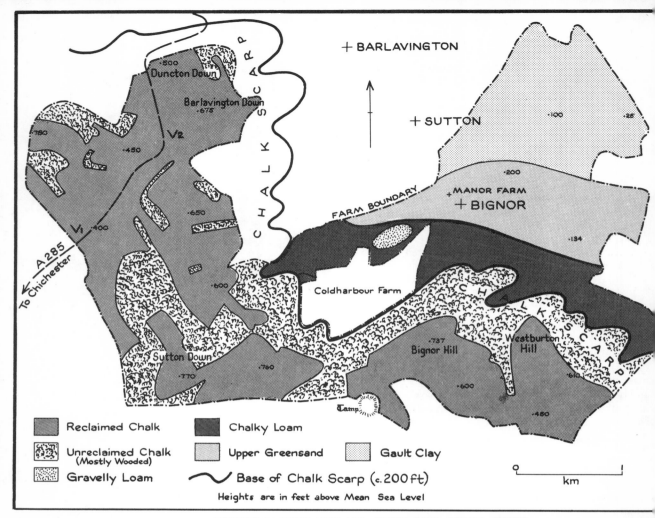

Heights are in feet above Mean Sea Level

CHANGES IN CHALK LAND USE: MANOR FARM, BIGNOR, SUSSEX.

*Manor Farm lies on the northern edge of the South Downs. It comprises 1053 hectares and includes segments of three rock outcrops (see map). The soils on the Upper Greensand and Lower Chalk have been cultivated for centuries, the latter soil having an admixture of residual clay 'sludge' derived from the steep chalk scarp (see diagram, p. **76**). Until recently the bulk of the chalk downland was covered by either rough pasture or scrub. Between 1900 and 1920, however, some 80 ha of chalkland was reclaimed in the valley V1–V2. The rest of the chalk reclamation took place between 1939 and 1969. Factors favouring reclamation include mechanization, the availability of improved fertil-izers, better and quicker-growing varieties of seeds and guaranteed prices. Mr. J. Tupper (the farmer to whom the author is indebted for this information) states that his chalk soils need heavy doses of fertilizers and are deficient in copper. He also stresses the heavy overhead costs of chalk cultivation resulting from incessant damage to tractor tyres and to implements generally, caused by innumerable flints. The Gault Clay land at the north-east end of the farm is cultivated but could be much improved by extensive drainage. This pattern of changing land use is similar all along the South Downs.*

40 minutes, and this is one important reason for the change in land use (*see also p.* 82). Similarly in South Island, New Zealand, many sheep-farms contain relatively inaccessible terrain which was formerly neglected: today it has been converted into intensive grazing land by means of aerial seeding, fertilizing and the dropping of fencing gear. Yet another advantage of improved rural transport is that it permits farm workers to live within reach of urban amenities although their place of work may be in remote country districts. This enables, for example, farm-workers on the bleak, dead-flat Ijssel Meer polders to enjoy a community existence in pleasant centrally placed towns like Emmeloord (*map p.* 68) instead of living in isolated cottages adjacent to the fields they till. In fact the mechan-ization of farming, coupled with improvements

in rural transport facilities, tends to lead to the curious situation where more townspeople than country people are employed, directly or indirectly, by agriculture.

An example of the impact of mechanization on peasant cultivation may be quoted from West Africa. Along the coast between the Rivers Gambia and Niger there are numerous treeless grasslands, where efforts are being made to increase agricultural production without undermining the traditional systems of semi-subsistence farming, or bringing about soil impoverishment or erosion. There are many difficulties to be overcome, including (i) the small, fragmented nature of each peasant's holding; (ii) the shifting methods of cultivation, whereby isolated clearings in bush and savana are soon exhausted and abandoned; (iii) the danger of triggering off disastrous soil erosion by introducing mechanized ploughs; (iv) the lack of capital and technical expertise among the peasants; (v) the high expense of clearing the land and of maintaining and supervising farm machinery; and (vi) finding annual cash crops which can be marketed at a price sufficiently high to make mechanization economically worth while. In three separate locations these problems are being tackled on a communal basis by setting up hire-contract units to operate farm machinery, and to supply fertilizers and seed. The general effect has been to stabilize farm units and improve crop yields.

Peasant farmers in those villages participating in the scheme concentrate the area which they wish to cultivate into a single block which is ploughed and discharrowed. The peasants then plant, tend and harvest cassava and okra (*Hibiscus esculens*), a popular vegetable. These crops do well in the dry conditions and have a ready sale in Accra and Tema. Ruling prices enable the peasants to meet the ploughing fees which are being gradually raised to an economic level. Green fallow crops are encouraged to maintain fertility instead of the area being allowed to revert to bush. Areas ploughed are mainly but not exclusively black clay.[1]

In coastal Sierra Leone there are extensive freshwater grass swamps, affected by seasonal inundation, but suitable for mechanized cultivation. Large portions of these swamps are now ploughed and disc-harrowed under contract and

are used by peasant farmers to grow rice. Swamp rice is also being grown farther inland in the *bolis* —flooded bottom-lands—of the gently undulating hill country, where the Department of Agriculture operates a mechanized cultivation scheme for the local farmers. Here fertilizers are drilled in with the seed to remedy soil deficiencies.

Because there is a sustained demand for rice, more could be done, provided there were machines, skilled mechanics and European supervisors available, and provided the farmers were willing to share in the effort and not simply to expect the work to be done at subsidized rates. Should these schemes succeed— and in spite of set-backs the signs are that many will do so—a most important step forward will have been taken in West African agriculture.[2]

Remarkable developments are also taking place in India, within the framework of the Intensive Agricultural Areas Programme. From 1960 to 1967 this scheme operated in one district of each of the seventeen Indian States. In these districts various improved mechanical devices for cultivation and food handling were introduced simultaneously, together with many supporting services such as banking and finance, fertilizer and seed supply (including hybrids), farm planning advice and education. As a result the consumption of fertilizers in the seventeen districts shot up from 76 000 tonnes to 528 000 tonnes, total farm inputs increased by more than 80 million rupees and the total value of farm produce marketed through co-operatives rose by more than sixfold. In fact the Programme was so successful that it has now been expanded to cover 130 districts and 10 per cent of India's cultivated area.

Results such as these are not yet the rule in the developing world. In many developing countries nothing more substantial than a barbed wire fence may separate a crop which would be creditable in an advanced system of farming from one which will yield not much more than a tenth as much. The 'maximum yield' plots of cotton at the experiment station at Samaru in Northern Nigeria always yield more than 2000 kg per hectare of seed cotton; the average yield in the area is perhaps 280 kg per hectare. In many regions we already know technically how at least to double or treble yields and where we do not, we know how to find out:

[1] H. P. White, 'Mechanized Cultivation of Peasant Holdings in West Africa', *Geography*, No. 202, p. 269.

[2] Ibid.

but to translate these abilities into practice on a large scale is another matter.[1]

Technical advances and rationalization in agriculture cannot alone solve the problems of underdeveloped countries, for such advances inevitably entail at least some movement of people out of farming. In the long run these displaced workers can be absorbed into new industrial and commercial enterprises, but meanwhile it may be necessary to provide them with simple manufacturing and processing equipment for use in their own homes. Similar problems of rural unemployment which affected Great Britain in the 18th century were eased by the development of 'cottage' or 'domestic' industries using unsophisticated hand-operated machines, but the comparison is by no means exact.

12. Storage, handling and processing

Storage, handling and processing methods vitally affect the proportion of harvested foodstuffs which ultimately gets consumed. Faulty handling methods at present result in huge losses, especially of grains, vegetables, fruits, animal products and fish. It has been estimated, for example, that about 10 per cent of all the world's stored grain is lost, and in the worst affected regions the proportion is as high as 50 per cent.[2] Stocks of food provide an ideal medium for the growth of moulds and bacteria, and provide nourishment for a multitude of such voracious pests as rats, mice, termites and weevils. Additional problems are posed by the 'breathing' or germation of seeds, chemical decomposition (e.g. of vegetable fats and oils), spontaneous combustion (e.g. of hay and other silage crops) and the bruising of fruit by rough handling. Food losses resulting from the action of micro-organisms and insects are greatly increased under conditions of warmth and high humidity. Thus it is absolutely vital that foodstuffs be stored in a dry and preferably cool environment, and that they be properly dry themselves before being stowed away. This presents serious problems in many underdeveloped countries, where the usual way of drying farm products is in the sun. In Latin America, for example, coffee beans are spread out to dry in the open air on mats or concrete floors, and similar methods are employed with West African cacao and yams, Melanesian copra, Assam tea and Monsoon Asian rice. In the latter case there is the special problem of the rice grains becoming damaged by cracking, but with all crops really effective sun-drying is difficult, especially where there is a protracted rainy season. Thus great savings could be brought about by the installation in the villages of backward rural regions of simple but effective drying and storage facilities, for use on a co-operative basis by farmers in the adjoining countryside. One effect would be greatly to increase the market quality of stored foods, especially of those which are harvested in the rainy season. In rice-growing countries this might well encourage farmers to sow a second crop of soya beans or groundnuts after the traditional rice harvest: at present many of them are put off by the low prices fetched by foodstuffs which are damp, damaged and soiled.

Simple storage sheds in the tropics must be so designed that they exclude rain and vermin, but are well ventilated to allow the free percolation of air: otherwise a drop in the temperature of the outside air can cause damaging condensation. Inside temperatures can be minimized by providing adequate insulation and ventilation of the roof. Control of humidity within storage buildings can be achieved by installing air-conditioning apparatus, but this method is too costly for general use in underdeveloped countries. Other devices designed to prevent foods deteriorating include refrigeration, dehydration, refining (either partial or complete) and the introduction of chemical preservatives. Machines for all these processes are expensive and their installation, operation and maintenance calls for the attention of trained technicians. There is also the added difficulty that these processes may adversely affect the food value and/or the palatability and hence the market value of the final product.

Considerable losses are incurred, notably in the less advanced countries, as a result of pre-

---

[1] A. H. Bunting and Alan Harrison, 'Improving Traditional Agriculture', *Science Journal*, May, 1968, p. 64.

[2] Walter H. Pawley, *op. cit.*, p. 127.

mature harvesting by poverty-stricken farmers who are desperately anxious to make a sale. Tropical crops which are often cut in an unripe condition include sugar cane, groundnuts, oil-palm, coconuts and cassava. The losses resulting from such premature harvesting only become apparent during processing, when the crops are found to yield abnormally low contents of sugar, vegetable oil or starch. An F.A.O. expert has calculated that in Siam alone more than 100 000 tonnes of sugar are lost annually by the harvesting of unripe cane. A somewhat similar loss of food potential is involved when farmers in Britain dig up their barely maturing late potatoes and sell them as 'spring earlies'—to cash in on a temporarily high market price. Losses are also incurred during the processing of foods, in the form of waste products or by-products which are unsuitable for human consumption. Examples include molasses and bagasse, the by-products of sugar refining, oilcake residues produced by the crushing of nuts and seeds to extract vegetable oils, and the husks remaining after grain has been milled. Some of these by-products can be used as animal feed or as fuel, but modern processing methods and machinery aim to keep the proportion of waste down to an absolute minimum. In vegetable oil refining, for example, the oil content of the cake residues produced with primitive equipment in West Africa is about 10 per cent, whereas modern expellers keep the oil content of the cakes down to about 4 per cent. Similar savings result from the use of modern equipment to refine sugar, mill grain, extract juices from fruits, remove peanuts from their shells, dry grapes and figs, process olives and dates, and so on. Where a country's economy is sufficiently advanced to allow farmers to take advantage of such modern methods of food preserving as canning, dehydration, refrigeration and pickling, they can ensure that their products will reach the market in a first-class, saleable condition and will fetch a sufficiently high price. This allows farmers to anticipate satisfactory profits and so encourages them to increase their output of market garden foods.

A useful example of how modern techniques of food processing and preservation, coupled with high-powered marketing and fast freight train deliveries, are helping greatly to expand the agricultural output of a region may be quoted from Languedoc (France). For centuries Languedoc has been famous for its wine. Indeed Hérault has two-thirds of its surface covered in vineyards and produces two-fifths of all French wine (most *vin ordinaire*). But many farms are too small for efficiency and much land suffers acutely from drought in summer. Furthermore, over-concentration on wine production has impoverished the soils and made the population too dependent on a single crop. However . . .

Something is stirring in France's 'Deep South'. From the lower Rhône almost to the Spanish frontier, a vast stretch of sunbaked land is being transformed into a bountiful fruit and vegetable garden. . . . Today an impressive network of dams, canals and irrigation ditches is reaching out across the region's 600 000-odd acres. By 1975, when the plan is complete, about 420 000 acres . . . will be under irrigation. The principal work is a 174′ wide canal carrying Rhône river water from a point north of Arles to Pézenas 100 miles away. . . . From this main waterway, more than 130 miles of tributary canals are being dug to link with farmers' pumps and sprinkler systems throughout the eastern half of the zone. For the west, the waters of the Orb and the Hérault are being harnessed. . . . Also under way . . . are . . . refrigerating centres, silos, slaughter houses, cattle-food factories, canning plants, markets, farm equipment and other ancillary industries. . . .

An increasing flow of apples and pears is finding its way to Paris, the Common Market countries and London. . . . Soon loads of peaches, apricots, plums, melons, asparagus, cauliflowers and potatoes, as well as better-quality wines, will be rolling out of the south-west. An up-to-the-minute co-operative marketing complex at Nîmes is already showing what can be done, with teleprinters flashing hourly reports on Covent Garden, Milan, Brussels, Paris and Hamburg.[3]

13. Land-holding and management

Land tenure and land distribution systems have profound effects upon the efficiency and

[3] *Daily Telegraph.*

productivity of farming. In many parts of the world, notably in underdeveloped regions such as the Middle and Far East and Latin America, agricultural holdings are very small and are frequently incapable of giving full employment to the families which occupy them. At the same time many farmers do not own the land which they cultivate. In many backward economies, for example, there is no conception of individual land ownership: an individual occupies his share of a communal holding, and also has a part interest in uncultivated but potentially useful land belonging to his group. An illustration may be taken from Syria, where village land called *much'a* is held in common by all the inhabitants but is cultivated in individual family plots. From time to time these plots are re-allotted among the cultivators, which gives them little or no incentive to improve the land which they work.

Communal rights prevent the energetic or able individual members of the group from acquiring more land at the expense of the indolent or unproductive. They also make it difficult, if not impossible for either an individual or the group to borrow on the security of land for such productive purposes as the purchase of fertilizers or of simple equipment. Individuals also are unlikely to spend much effort or money on improving cultivated plots when these are periodically re-allotted by the tribal or village authorities, as often happens. The system tends to encourage uneconomic farming practices in other ways. For example, there is no incentive to the individual to limit the number of cattle he grazes on communal land, since any benefit is likely to be reduced by the over-grazing practised by others. Similarly, the improvement in the quality of cattle is retarded if different herds are grazed together. The system may also discourage economically sound conservation practices . . . if the benefits would be shared by all the communal owners while only some of them would be willing to contribute to the cost of the required improvements.[1]

In Monsoon Asia, Latin America and parts of southern Europe a system of land tenure known as *métayage* is very widespread. In its simplest form this is a co-partnership between the owner, who provides land, buildings, equipment and seed, and the *métayer*, who provides labour and stock in return for a fixed share of the

1 Peter T. Bauer and Basil S. Yamey, *The Economics of Under-developed Countries*, Nisbet and C.U.P., p. 52.

produce. Systems of *métayage* vary greatly in detail, but a feature common to them all is that the people who actually work the land have only an indirect control over their earnings and usually find it very difficult to improve their lot. The following account of *métayage* in Italy is typical of many land tenure arrangements in southern Europe:

At the top of the scarp east of Arezzo is a plateau nearly 2700 ft. above sea-level, covered with only a sparse vegetation of withered grass and scrub in spite of the mean rainfall of some 32 in. a year. The summer drought is more serious here than in Lombardy or Emilia, especially as the soils are very poor and thin. One of the *métayers* who farms in this region has about 125 acres, and his house stands isolated in the midst of his fields. Thirty-five acres are arable, and only $7\frac{1}{2}$ of these have rows of vines. The latter give 40 cwt. of grapes, which yield 290 gallons of wine, but the *métayer's* share is hardly enough for the needs of his own family. Lower down, on the scarp, a few olive trees provide about 65 lb. of oil, which represents no more than a three-month supply for the family of three men, three women, and four children.

He has $12\frac{1}{2}$ acres of wheat land under the traditional grain-fallow rotation, and on it he sows 14 cwt. of seed to reap about 80 cwt. in a good year. Again, there is no surplus when he receives his share. Indeed, in drought years, he has to buy back a few sacks of grain to feed his family, During the second course of the rotation, apart from the fallow land, he grows a little over 1 acre of maize and about the same of barley and oats, which altogether provide a further 10–16 cwt. of grain. . . . His only dependable income is from his three flocks. As in nearby Corsica, each must have a herdsman to ensure that the animals make the most of the sparse grazing. For draught purposes he keeps two cows, which are sold after five or six years of use, and he rears a pair of heifers to replace them. . . .

Hunger is the immediate result of a poor wheat or vine harvest. As for the building, its roof is sadly in need of repair, and the family still depend on candles or oil-lamps for light. It is not surprising that they want to move. The owner, 'a grasping and unintelligent person' according to Dr. Lombardi of the Arezzo Agricultural Inspectorate, lives in Arezzo on the revenue from six similar holdings. It is many a long year since he spent anything on them even for maintenance. On this particular holding the *métayer* has no wheelbarrow, and so the manure is taken from the sheds and sheep-folds on a kind of stretcher carried by two men. As the family obtain so little from their crops, they waste their time gleaning their fields and collecting all kinds of produce for fodder, from oak twigs and reeds to leaves from various plants, including the clematis. Similar use is made of holly leaves on the Lanvaux heathlands in Morbihan.

The agreement . . . between the landowners and the *métayers* allotted 47 per cent of the harvest to the farmers, who are also responsible for half the expenses. The *métayer* in question thus retains only 53 per cent of the drop yields enumerated above, and these are in any case . . . inferior. . . . Even when the family have poultry on their table, they have to make a 'compulsory gift' to the proprietor.[2]

Systems of *métayage* sometimes involve pure 'share-cropping', i.e. there is no fixed rent, but the tenant cultivates the land and gives the owner a share—often 50 per cent—of the agricultural produce. This system gives the tenant some protection from fluctuations in harvests and crop prices and is usually preferable to fixed cash tenancies in which a tenant tends to fall progressively deeper into debt whenever the income from his crops falls below the outgoing rent. The traditional method of covering the deficit is by having recourse to a moneylender—a role performed for centuries by Jews in Europe, Greeks in the Middle East, Chinese in Southeast Asia and by the *banjas* in India. In backward rural regions moneylenders often charge exorbitant rates of interest and wield considerable power: witness the manner in which the word *banja* is used in India as a vitriolic term of abuse.

Métayage is an archaic system which almost always loads the dice in favour of the owner as against the *métayer*. Professor Dumont[2] regards it as being 'appropriate only to regions lacking in both technical knowledge and capital and harassed by a high density of rural population . . . but to condemn a region irrevocably to *métayage* would . . . bar the way to further progress'. One major snag in the system is the incessant battle between owner and tenant concerning such items as the sale and prices of crops and livestock, the list of products to be shared, the duration of contracts, the exact responsibilities of the owner

2 René Dumont, op. cit., p. 244.

in the maintenance of farm equipment and the owner's right to give notice. Lack of security of tenure by the *métayer* is a particularly serious brake on productivity, for a tenant is unlikely to spend money on improvements if he is in constant fear of eviction. Reform of the system is very difficult, however, for rationalization and mechanization inevitably creates added unemployment. Furthermore, examples in southern Europe show that where landowners have bequeathed their land to *métayers*, yields have tended to fall due to a lack of workshops, tractors, communal services, capital and managerial expertise, all of which were formerly provided by the more enlightened owners. Recent experience with the *Cassa per il Mezzogiorno* (Fund for the South) in southern Italy suggests that the only effective path towards reform lies through such techniques as voluntary or State-organized co-operatives, able to supply equipment, knowledge, assured markets and some form of agricultural processing or light engineering industries to absorb displaced farm-workers.

In parts of southern Europe and Latin America, small, intensively worked overpopulated farm plots exist side by side with enormous privately owned estates, on which there may be little or no cultivation even though the land is fertile. Some large estates in southern Spain, for example, are devoted almost entirely to the rearing of bulls destined for the arena, whilst on others most of the land is reserved for hunting and shooting. Generally speaking, land on the large estates (*latifundia*) is used very extensively: on some of them, for example, the main resource is still the wild scrub and steppe, and animals are raised mostly on unimproved grazing land. Where the land is ploughed a simple type of rotation is employed involving one or two years of grazed fallow, so that cereal yields rarely exceed 1·25 tonnes or so per hectare. The alienation of huge tracts of useful land from effective cultivation is most marked in Latin America, where medieval European systems of land tenure were introduced by the Conquistadores, and where the control of land has traditionally been associated with social prestige, and with political and economic power.

Large-scale agricultural enterprises, with the control of work opportunities vested in the hands of a few land-owning families or corporations, is still characteristic of great areas. The land-holding classes of Latin America, schooled in traditions of *land* as a symbol of prestige, are given to speculative production on the one hand and to the practice of maintaining large tracts of idle but inaccessible land on the other. Land resources of the region have been diminishing for centuries, because of inefficient methods of cultivation such as fire agriculture, lack of fertilizers, deforestation, erosion, etc. At the same time the concentration in ownership, often without full use of the land, has aggravated the problems of land pressure.... The failure (of Latin America) to make the most effective use of its total immense area is closely related to the system of land-use, settlement and of land-tenure which prevail.[1]

Within Latin America efforts to reform the land tenure system associated with *latifundia* have been most effective in Mexico, and the method adopted there has frequently been extolled as a model for action elsewhere. It entails the establishment by Governmental decree of a multitude of *ejidos*, each *ejido* consisting of

a community or village, together with its communal lands granted to the community by the Federal Government of Mexico.[2]

The *ejido* system was first introduced in Mexico in 1917, following many years of revolutionary turmoil during which the main grievances of the people concerned the alienation of the vast majority of them from land ownership, and the social and economic injustices inherent in the *latifundia* pattern of land use—or misuse. Within each *ejido* there are usually 20–100 families, and each family is allowed to cultivate, but not own, 10 hectares of irrigable land or 20 hectares of non-irrigable land. This right to cultivation is inherited by the wife or eldest son

of a family, but the land may not be sold, rented, mortgaged, given away, or the right to occupancy be modified in any way. Forest and pasture land within an *ejido* remains strictly communal. In fact the formation of *ejidos* involves the restoration of a system of landholding villages which the original Spanish settlers established alongside the *latifundia*. Through the centuries the owners of the *latifundia* gradually eroded the village system, often seizing the villagers' land by force, so that by the early 20th century the overwhelming majority of Mexicans were landless. The *ejido* legislation of 1917, which still forms the basis of Mexican land reform, affirms the right of each peasant to a parcel of land, invalidates the ownership of illegally seized village lands and puts a limit on the size of private estates. Private landowners who lose parts of their estates during the formation of *ejidos* are compensated with Government bonds of dubious worth.

At first the pace of Mexican land reform was slow, but it gathered such rapid momentum under President Lazaro Cardenas in 1934 that *ejido* land tenure is today the single most important class in Mexico and this novel type of Mexican land reform has certainly curtailed, if not broken, the political and economic stranglehold of wealthy private landowners and has given large numbers of formerly landless labourers a stake in the soil. On the other hand Mexican agriculture has suffered disappointing drops in productivity since the *ejidos* were established.

For example, on lands devoted to intensive cultivation of horticultural crops, value of production per hectare on *ejido* lands is reported to be 749 pesos compared with 1512 pesos per hectare on private lands; the gross income per man-year of work on *ejido* land totalled 4607 pesos compared with 10 795 pesos on private lands. Although the reasons are complicated, the lesser productivity is a symptom of the major problems of the *ejido* as it exists today. These major problems include (1) inadequate capital and credit, (2) excessive fragmentation of land, and (3) resulting difficulties in implementing agricultural science and technology.[3]

1 United Nations Report on Latin America.

2 J. Granville Jensen, *The Ejido in Mexico, A Contrast in Land Tenure*, Case Studies in World Geography, ed. Richard M. Highsmith, Jr., Prentice-Hall.

3 J. Granville Jensen, op. cit.

Hacienda de San Martin

km

Pueblo de +
Almoloya de Juarez

EJIDOS IN 1936

EJIDOS IN 1950

PRIVATE

In particular the *ejidatarios* (farmers) cannot borrow money in the normal way because they cannot pledge the land they work as security. To overcome this problem the Government created a special Ejidal Bank, empowered to grant loans, and to supply seeds, fertilizers and equipment to organized groups, of *ejidatarios*. This step led to a considerable amount of land improvement but did nothing to solve another basic snag—the fact that the *ejidatarios*' plots are so small that they tend inevitably to perpetuate rural under-employment and poverty.

Perhaps the most significant result of the lack of capital and small size is in the impairment of applications of modern agricultural science and technology. The practice of dividing the *ejido* into family rights created over two million *ejido* farm operators, many unprepared for land management, with little knowledge of modern agriculture, without capital, and generally with too little land. Against this multitude on the land, implementation of modern agricultural science and technology is dissipated in sheer numbers. Much is being done, but the needs are gargantuan and inadequate support is provided for the essential service of field agricultural assistance. . . . The *ejido*, symbol of the agrarian revolution, is a unique land-tenure system and its impact on the landscape and economy of Mexico is far reaching. Through its development the feudal system of the great *haciendas* has been ended and *camposinos* (peasants) in large numbers provided with land and freedom. There will be no easy or quick solution to the problems and improvements will be frustratingly slow. Nevertheless, the future well-being of Mexico depends in large measure on how the agrarian problem of the *ejido* is handled.[4]

In Europe the social and economic problems resulting from the *latifundia* system have been tackled most persistently and effectively in Italy, notably in the lower Po delta, Sicily, Sardinia, southern peninsular Italy and the Maremma. The latter comprises the coastal lowlands between Leghorn and Rome, a region which until recently was dominated by large estates largely given over to extensive sheep- and cattle-rearing on unimproved grazing lands. Traditionally the Maremma has been virtually a wasteland, a malarial infested region of swamps and inferior pasture, with a relatively scanty population but a

history of rural unemployment and malnutrition. Today, as a result of two decades of land reforms, the landscape has been radically altered. Formerly the Maremma contained 800 estates larger than 100 hectares, 80 000 farms smaller than 10 hectares and 7026 farms of 10–100 hectares, these categories of landholdings occupying 73·5 per cent, 10·9 per cent and 15·6 per cent of the total land area, respectively. Today all but the most efficient estates of over 365 hectares have been broken up, the former owners being allowed to keep one-third of their land (provided they engage in land improvement schemes), and the remaining two-thirds being taken over by the State. Compensation, as in Mexico, is in the form of State bonds. Of the confiscated land 40 per cent has been allocated to formerly landless labourers (*braccianti*) so that they can improve their lot by growing some food for themselves, or to peasants who owned plots of land which were too small for economic working; the remaining 60 per cent has been used to establish independent family farms. These reforms have been accompanied by a variety of schemes designed to improve productivity, including soil conservation, drainage, the planting of olives and vineyards, road construction, digging new wells and putting in piped water supply. New farm units, mostly about 10 hectares in extent, are provided with farm buildings and equipment and are designed to be worked by and to support an average family of seven. It is reckoned that such a farm needs four labour units, in which men rate as 1 unit, and children 12–16, old men over 60 and women all rate as $\frac{1}{2}$ unit. One-half of the capital cost of equipping a farm is a free gift from the State, and the remainder is repaid by the occupier over a period of thirty years at a low rate of interest of $3\frac{1}{2}$ per cent. At the end of thirty years the land becomes the property of the occupier. For the first three years of cropping a new farmer is on probation and must show a profit. To act as an example and as a stimulant to effective farming techniques, every twelfth farm is worked as a 'pilot plot' by experienced farmers mostly recruited from northern Italy. All resettled farmers are obliged to use specially set-up communal services for mechanical cultivation and for the marketing of farm produce. In addition each 8000 hectares of new land is supervised by a government agricultural scientist. Livestock is being improved by crossing the local

4 Ibid.

Maremma herds with other selected Italian beef breeds such as the Chianina. On the arable land the farmers are obliged to follow a seven-year rotation of beans/wheat/fallow/grain/lucerne/lucerne/wheat or a silage crop: this rotation has been specially designed gradually to eliminate fallow, concentrate on fodder crops and thus intensify livestock farming throughout the region. The whole Maremma scheme is underpinned by massive financial and technical assistance provided by the Italian government.

As in Mexico, land reform in Italy was precipitated by social unrest and acute political instability. In 1947, for example, armed bands of *braccianti* wandered about the countryside threatening to take over by force the idle land on *latifundia*. As in Mexico, too, the main criticism of the reforms is that they have tended to produce very large numbers of farm units that are too small for economic exploitation. The reason is that the scheme has concentrated on creating a class of land-owning peasants as a deliberate political move to combat Communism, so that economic efficiency has not been a prime aim. Today it is increasingly realized that land reform must be integrated into a general scheme in which mechanization plays a vital role and in which displaced farm-workers are absorbed into growing industries. One indication of the complexity of land reform involves the location of rural settlements. Traditionally many Italian farm-workers live in huge villages of 10 000–40 000 inhabitants, often located on remote hilltop sites, from which they spend hours each day walking up to 8 kilometres to and from their place of work. Recent Italian development plans have specifically aimed at dispersing workpeople in hamlets and individual farm dwellings. Now there is a growing body of opinion which recommends the regrouping of farm-workers in central townships: the reason being that many workers find isolation irksome and miss the companionship and social amenities of communal living.

It is indeed paradoxical that at the same time that small independent farm plots—many of them apparently too small to be economically viable—are being deliberately created in certain parts of the world, vigorous efforts are being made elsewhere towards farm consolidation. The countries of western Europe, in particular, are at present involved in an agricultural reorganization designed to adapt a basically peasant type of farming to the highly competitive commercial conditions of an advanced economy. Farm holdings which are too fragmented to be worked efficiently, or are too small, even when consolidated, to yield an adequate livelihood to their occupier, are gradually being eradicated. Fragmented holdings are very numerous in Western Europe partly due to the fact that much land was formerly cultivated on a communal open-field system, and the patterns of the strips into which the great open fields were divided became 'fossilized'. Other reasons for the minute subdivision of land include the splitting up of estates on inheritance; the piecemeal winning of wasteland from bog, heath and forest; growing population pressures on limited land resources, especially in the Mediterranean lands; and, in difficult terrain, the need to ensure that each farmer has a share of the best land available. Consolidation schemes vary in scope and scale from simple exchanges of plots of land to form larger but still separated holdings, to massive programmes of regional rationalization. In the latter case the scattered plots are amalgamated to form single compact holdings surrounding the farmsteads, field divisions are kept to a minimum,

An example of extreme fragmentation of farmland in West Germany. The elongated shape of the individual strips makes mechanized cultivation difficult.

106

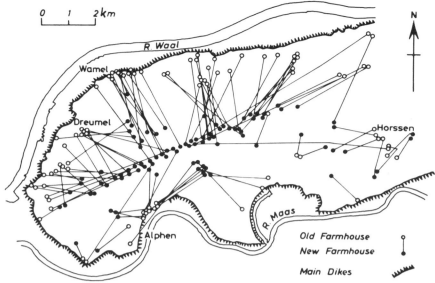

Old Farmhouse
New Farmhouse
Main Dikes

(Above) *The effect of farm consolidation on settlement: relocation of farms in the Land van Maas en Waal West, Netherlands. With the improvement of soils, drainage and communications farms have been moved from the dyke-side to the newly consolidated holdings in the centre of the basin-clay region between the dykes. Based on map in* Netherland Consolidation Commission Report 1957.

(Below) *Plan of field patterns before and after consolidation in the Serooskerke-Gapinge district on the island of Walcheren, Netherlands. Based on maps in the* Annual Report 1957 *of the Herverkavelings-commissie Walcheren. The various shadings show how individual specimen holdings have been reshaped.*

and the holdings are large enough to be managed efficiently and to give the farmers and their families an adequate level of living. In many Western European countries consolidation schemes form part of overall plans to improve farming efficiency by such means as improved drainage, water conservation, irrigation, soil conservation, more scientific tillage, boulder removal, making new roads and access ways, as well as the construction of new farm buildings and the establishment of rural industries.

Fragmentation is especially acute in France. In Savoy, for example,

... a typical mountain farm ... of barely 10 ha consisted of 275 parcels; a village of 828 ha in Loir-et-Cher had 5075 plots, while extreme

Old situation   New situation

The effect of farm consolidation on communications.
(Left) Savognin, Canton Valais, Switzerland, before consolidation. Only two tracks traverse the steep north-facing slope down to the river Julia. After consolidation (right) five access ways serve the same area, and farms can be worked more efficiently. The disappearance of some of the scrubby woodland and the reclamation of riverside land indicate more intensive use of the land.

cases exist in which a holding consists of a few square metres, a grape vine or a single olive tree.[1]

The minute size of many French land-holding units is in many cases the direct result of the break-up of large feudal estates under the Napoleonic Code Civil of 1803, which required an inheritance to be equally divided. During the past two decades consolidation has progressed at an accelerating rate, affecting some 5 million ha. At present the process in France is being completed at a rate of some 600 000 ha annually, but it will still require another twenty years to finish work on the outstanding 13 million ha of fragmented land. Consolidation is also taking place at a fast pace in Western Germany (about 260 000 ha p.a.), Italy (100 000 ha p.a.), Austria (60 000 ha p.a.), Sweden and Finland (each 50 000 ha p.a.), the Netherlands and Norway (each 45 000 ha p.a.), and at a slower but notable rate in Greece, Ireland and Switzerland. In Britain and Denmark consolidation was largely achieved by the end of the 19th century, but in Spain and Portugal, where there remain almost 3 million ha of fragmented farm plots,

[1] Dr. Audrey M. Lambert, 'Farm Consolidation in Western Europe', *Geography*, No. 218.

progress is very slow. Some idea of the scale and complexity of the problem both in Europe and elsewhere can be gained from the following quotations:[2]

Today 46 per cent of all Swiss farms need consolidation, the average holding comprising at least ten separate plots. The most severely fragmented cantons are those of Valais, Grisons and Ticino. In the Val Blenio, Ticino, two communes totalling 2200 ha were divided into 88 000 plots, held by 656 owners, an average of 134 plots per owner.

In Cyprus trees and buildings are often the property of persons other than the landowner, while water is owned separately from the land and trees which benefit from it. Further, many plots are held in undivided shares, so that in one case a property of less than £10 registered value was held in 369 lots involving 1912 co-owners.

In Portugal, where fully half the farmland requires consolidation, little has so far been achieved. Fragmentation, most serious in the north-western provinces where there are locally over 500 holdings to the square kilometre, gives rise to fields so small that a cow feeding on one man's land dungs his neighbour's plot.

[2] Dr. Audrey M. Lambert, loc. cit.

But farm consolidation is not restricted to Western Europe alone. Problems of fragmentation occur also in the communist lands of eastern Europe where state-sponsored communal or collective farms seek to overcome its obvious disadvantages. Nor is fragmentation lacking in other continents. It is a major impediment to economic advance in the densely peopled lands of Asia and consolidation legislation has been passed in Pakistan, India (Uttar Pradesh), Malaya and Japan to name but a few examples, while the productivity of the Chinese communes is constantly in the news. In Africa communal systems of land tenure and fragmentation of holdings underlie much political unrest . . . the problem is widespread in Central and South America. . . . In French Canada, division among heirs has splintered the 'ladder' farms along the St. Lawrence, while in the U.S.A. fragmentation occurs not only in the Great Lakes cut-over region and the southern Appalachians but even in the mid-west where holdings consisting of several discrete blocks are now in evidence.

Fragmentation of land holdings is a world-wide problem; farm consolidation in Western Europe is one attempt at a solution. The need to maximize farm efficiency is urgent in face of the growing world population. Mechanization can help, but since the tractor is for agriculture what the steam engine was for the Industrial Revolution, larger and more efficient farm units are first essentials. Whether the increased productivity which should result from farm consolidation will develop rapidly to meet the political and economic needs of the world's population explosion remains to be seen.

It is worth noting that although Great Britain is not faced with land tenure and land fragmentation problems of the same magnitude as many other countries, difficulties do exist, especially within the English Midlands, where inefficiency in farming can often be traced back to impractical farm shapes. Among the findings of an official survey[3] of certain Midland parishes it is noted that:

1. The higher standards of farming were to be found on the farms which were largest in size, had the best farm layouts, the better buildings and the more straightforward owner-occupier relationships.

2. A measurement devised to know the degree of convenience in farm layouts showed that only 23 farms out of 66 could be classed as 'good'.

3. The state of land ownership was very complex. With the exception of a few large estates, the farms were held by owner-occupiers . . . or by tenants who had difficulties arising from impecunious landlords and divided ownership. Any attempts to alter farm size and layout without altering the ownership would just make the tenure pattern even more complex and unsatisfactory.

On a national scale a government survey[4] suggests that about 25 per cent of holdings (i.e. 70 000 holdings) in England and Wales have their land severed in one or more places. Most of these fragmented holdings exist in the old Anglo-Saxon areas of England, where detached plots —formerly won from the 'waste'—are linked to farms which have their farmsteads within nucleated villages. The *Survey* judges that at least one-half of all English and Welsh farms larger than 2 hectares have a layout which is 'bad' or 'only fair', and further suggests that there appears to be a very high correlation between the efficiency and productivity of a farm and its situation, layout and method of land tenure.

Many questions, to which we do not know the answers, arise when thinking about this problem. To what extent is the best use of land within rural Britain being prevented by the accident of its occupation and ownership? A degree of extra cost in food production must arise through bad farm layouts, size and provision of fixed equipment. How serious is it? How does it compare with the probable administrative and other costs of attempting improvements in farm shape and size through democratic process? Are we reaching the limit of effectiveness of technical improvements in farm husbandry because of these rigidities and faults of the physical farming structure? If so, where exactly are the areas and how high is their farming potential if reallocation of land was carried out? . . .

Here in Britain, there has been no awakening of national or local conscience on the problem, and the first attempt to suggest a voluntary rearrangement of farm land in a small area in Dorset has foundered amidst a welter of legal and administrative difficulties and both local and national opposition.[5]

[3] A. L. S. Research Group, *A Study of the Agricultural Structure of Four Midland Parishes*, unpublished report, Ministry of Agriculture and Food, 1951.

[4] *National Farm Survey of England and Wales, A Summary Report*, H.M.S.O.

[5] Dr. G. P. Wibberley, 'Some Aspects of Problem Rural Areas in Britain', *Geographical Journal*, Vol. CXX, Part I, p. 56.

Section 4. **Unconventional and synthetic foods**

14. New sources of protein

Protein deficiency is a major cause of malnutrition in all of the world's underdeveloped territories. In India, for example, the *per capita* protein supply in the daily diet is about 50 g, whereas 70 g per day are required to prevent a deficiency condition in adults.

> The lower income groups of the population, who form a large majority, get an even smaller quantity of protein in their diet. Children below the age of five years, who are growing fast and require body-building protein in sufficient quantities (two grammes per kilogramme body weight a day) are the worst sufferers. About 80 per cent of them suffer to varying degrees from protein malnutrition. *Kwashiorkor* and *marasmus*, the main syndromes of protein malnutrition, can be found in almost every village and among the slum dwellers of the cities. In many cases, low income combined with non-availability of low-cost protein foods and lack of knowledge about nutrition are the main causes. The average *per capita* consumption of milk in India is only 110 g a day and the position is equally serious in many other less developed countries.[1]

One attempt currently being made by scientists to counter this acute problem involves tapping unconventional sources of protein, notably those contained in oilseed meals. The meals under investigation are mainly residues produced during the extraction of vegetable oils from soya beans, peanuts and cottonseed. Hitherto these meals have been widely used to make cattle 'cake', but not human food because they are deficient in certain amino acids, especially methionine and lysine, and sometimes they contain toxic matter.

[1] Dr. H. A. B. Parpia, Director of the Central Food Technological Research Institute, *Science Journal*, May, 1968.

Research has therefore concentrated on two main objectives, namely, (i) improving methods of vegetable-oil refining so that the meal is free of contamination by oil solvents and other toxic residues such as oxalic acid and gossypol; and (ii) the search for ready supplies of amino acids which can be added to the meal. Both lines of research have recently proved fruitful: for example a very potent toxin in peanuts, produced by a mould, *Aspergillus flavus*, can be eliminated by spraying the growing crops with a mixture of phosphene and ammonia; and amino acids can be added to the meal by mixing in quantities of grain legumes such as broad beans and lentils, which are particularly rich in lysine. Amino acids can also be synthesized: in fact synthetic lysine and methionine are already being sold at very competitive prices.

Edible mixtures of oilseed meal and legumes have recently appeared on the market, mainly in Latin America and India, and many more will be available in the near future. These preparations, providing they are palatable and acceptable as staple foodstuffs, could do enormous good in combating protein deficiency.

In India a concentrated food called Indian Multipurpose Food Supplement has been developed which consists of 75 per cent edible grade peanut flour and 25 per cent chickpea flour. It is fortified with vitamins and minerals and its protein content is about 42 per cent. The product has been extensively tried and offers very good scope for use under Indian conditions. The country has 16 distinct cultural groups, each with its own food habits, and it is extremely difficult to develop special products for all of them. The Indian Multipurpose Food Supplement has therefore been adopted for inclusion in a few hundred traditional receipes for daily consumption so that there is no need for any daily change in food habits. Five manufacturing plants have been set up in India for its production. One of the

States has been using the supplement regularly in its school midday meal programme at the rate of about two tonnes a day for the past six years, and a number of industrial centres are showing a keen interest in using it to supplement the diet of their workers. It has also been used successfully in the famine distressed areas of the country recently and in the treatment of children suffering from malnutrition. The product has the advantage that it can be manufactured by any of the existing oil mills with small amount of extra equipment.[2]

Peanut flour is also being used to supplement the protein content of wheaten flour. In India a peanut-wheat flour mix, containing protein concentrate, vitamins and minerals, is being used to make 'Nutro-Biscuits', as a normal item of food for children. In India, too, a protein-rich, rice-shaped grain consisting of 60 per cent tapioca flour, 15 per cent groundnut flour and 25 per cent wheat flour is gaining success as a rice-substitute. There are also various Indian 'toned-milk' powders containing a mixture of animal milk and vegetable milk, the latter being derived from peanuts. The vegetable milk proportion in some of these powders is as high as 74 per cent, but

... feeding trials carried out by the Christian Medical Hospital, Vellore, indicate that there is no significant difference between the height and weight of the children fed with this product and those fed with a milk based product. The cost of this spray dried milk substitute will be only about 60 per cent of the cost of a product based on animal milk .... will increase the milk supply four times ... and be within the reach of the lower income group.[3]

Other possible future sources of protein for inclusion in human food include sunflower, mustard, rape and linseed—the use of all of which is at present excluded by an inability to get rid of toxic matter. Promising experiments are also in progress to produce high-protein foods from alfalfa grass. According to Dr. Parpia,

... protein malnutrition could be overcome over much of the world if the available resources of oilseed protein were utilized more

efficiently and were supplemented with grain legumes and amino acids. The prices of most of these products could be several times less than those of animal proteins. Furthermore the use of this vegetable protein is also attractive inasmuch as a given area of land can produce six times as much vegetable protein as animal protein. ... What is urgently required is a vigorous educational and marketing campaign, through public agencies and also through the private marketing organizations, to meet the consumers' requirements with non-conventional plant protein products in the form of traditional preparations. Weaning foods, biscuits, ice cream, beverages and sweets can all be made from cheaply obtained vegetable protein. If we are to avoid the possibilities of even greater future famines, these new and unconventional food products will have to be exploited as soon as possible.[4]

One very unconventional source of high-quality protein is the group of unicellular organisms. This group includes bacteria, yeasts, fungi, and algae, all of which are amenable to controlled growth. If 'crops' of such organisms are washed and dried the end product is an edible powder consisting of dead cells containing 35–75 per cent protein: such a powder is known colloquially as SCP, for single-cell protein. For the propagation of SCP organisms it is necessary to prepare a substrate ('culture solution') upon which the organisms can 'feed'. The main ingredients of the substrate are either carbohydrates or hydrocarbons, plus smaller quantities of nitrogen, magnesium, sulphur, phosphorus, some trace elements, air and water. One great advantage of SCP as a potential source of food is that carbohydrates and hydrocarbons are already produced in vast quantities as waste residues in various industrial processes, especially in the refining of vegetable and mineral oils. Examples of such by-products include molasses, kerosene, distillate oil and methane. Another advantage is that SCP organisms grow faster, and convert their inputs of 'feed' into edible products more efficiently, than any other food source. Furthermore all SCP powders, unlike many plant proteins, are rich in lysine, and some also contain adequate supplies of other important amino acids such as methionine and tryptophan. SCP could therefore be used to very good effect either as a complete source of protein or as a protein supplement to boost the nutrient value of staple

[2] Dr. H. A. B. Parpia, op. cit.
[3] Ibid.
[4] Ibid.

foods such as wheat, soya beans, maize and rice—all of which are deficient in amino acids.

For large-scale production of SCP

> ...bacteria and yeasts seem more suitable than fungi and algae, which grow more slowly and are less efficient in converting either nitrogen or carbon into protein. Fungi and algae are also considerably lower in protein content and appear to have more marked deficiencies in essential amino acids than bacteria or yeasts. The cell wall of fungi and algae constitutes a greater fraction of the cell, and will presumably furnish only roughage. The problems arising from the production of toxic secondary products are at least as great for bacteria and yeasts. The only significant advantage that filamentous fungi and algae possess is that they can be recovered from the fermentation broths by relatively simple operations such as string filtration, whereas for bacteria and yeasts more expensive means such as centrifugation will probably be required.[1]

Research to find the most satisfactory substrates with which to cultivate SCP is currently being carried out by various oil companies including Esso (in conjunction with Nestlé), Shell and British Petroleum. The latter company is building a large SCP plant at Lavéra (Marseilles) which will have an annual output of 16 000 tonnes by 1970. This plant will use as a substrate the higher paraffins derived from mineral-oil refining. Esso-Nestlé are using a purified paraffin substrate and Shell rely on methane. All the evidence suggests that hydrocarbons are preferable to carbohydrates for this purpose, mainly because the former

> ...are available in very large quantities as non-agricultural products. Thus, their production will not vary with climatic variations; there will not be problems associated with the education of farmers; prices should be relatively stable; and the amount of hydrocarbon actually needed for SCP production should have little impact on the overall hydrocarbon supply situation.[2]

Large-scale, economic production of SCP is feasible in the foreseeable future, but before it could be used as a staple food it would have to be put on the market in an acceptable, palatable and attractive form. This involves serious problems concerning its colour, flavour, solubility and compatibility with conventional foods, as well as exhaustive tests to ensure that it contained no toxic properties.

For SCP to have a significant impact on world nutrition would require the production and distribution of millions of tonnes of final product each year. If we are to take a lesson from history, specifically that of oilseed meals and fish protein concentrates, the most important barriers to distribution will be those related to social eating patterns, government regulations and the technological status of local food industries in less-developed countries. It is reasonable to predict that at least the economic and technological problems of SCP production will be overcome within the coming decade. The torch will then have been passed to the social scientists, the marketing and distribution people and the statesmen.[3]

The question remains whether the purely chemical synthesis of nutritional molecules will ever be practicable on a scale large enough effectively to relieve world food shortages. The technological problems involved in this branch of applied chemistry are already well on the way to solution, and so the answer mainly depends on whether such foods can be made cheap enough to compete economically with foods produced by conventional methods of husbandry. Synthetic food additives are already sold in considerable quantities, notably in the form of vitamin pills. These contain substances which are vital to human health, such as riboflavin and ergosterol, and can be used medicinally to correct dietary deficiencies in persons suffering from illness or malnutrition. Synthetic vitamins are also used widely as supplements to infant foods, certain staples such as margarine, bread and polished rice, and in animal feeding-stuffs. It has already been noted (*page 110*) that certain amino acids, e.g. lysine and methionine, are also relatively easy to synthesize and these, too, are increasingly being used as food 'fillers'. According to Dr. Magnus Pyke,

> It has been estimated that, provided a sufficiently large demand should arise, it would be possible to synthesize any of the L-amino acids for 2.00–8.00 dollars a kilogramme. The usefulness of achieving this scientific and

[1] S. R. Tannenbaum and R. I. Mateless, 'Single Cell Protein', *Science Journal*, May 1968.
[2] S. R. Tannenbaum, op. cit.
[3] Ibid.

technological feat will depend on the cost of protein in natural food, the possibility of synthesizing amino acids by microbiological fermentation or of breeding crops to contain an increased concentration of amino acids in which they are naturally deficient—this has already been achieved with great success with maize, of which hybrids rich in lysine have been developed.[4]

Hitherto the only synthetic food to be produced on a commercial scale is fat. This was synthesized by German chemists during the Second World War, under the pressure of severe food shortages. Although the German factories went out of production in 1945 there is no doubt that such fat can serve as a major food supplement.

Synthetic flavouring agents are also widely used. Diacetyl bears a resemblance to the taste of butter, methyl-3-methylthiopropionate to that of pineapple, decanal to that of orange, propyl acetate to that of pear and gamma-undecalactone to that of peach. The tastes of onion and garlic are given by ethyl thiocyanate and diallyl disulphide and that of coconut by gamma-nonalactone, while the synthetic organic compound, saccharin, has long been used as a substitute for the natural organic compound, sucrose (common sugar) as a source of sweetness. . . . . food can undoubtedly be synthesized in chemical factories at a price. Meanwhile, we can expect the existing market for synthetic vitamins and amino acids, flavouring agents and non-foods to grow. Synthetic fats, proteins and carbohydrates will come into their own when they can compete— as synthetic rubber can—with biologically produced supplies. And this may not be so very far in the future.[5]

15. Aquatic foods & fish farming

Close attention is also being given to the possibility of greatly expanding the use of aquatic animals and plants as foodstuffs. At

[4] Magnus Pyke, 'Synthetic Foods', *Science Journal*, May, 1968.
[5] Magnus Pyke, loc. cit.

present the total annual world catch of marine fish (including crustaceans and molluscs) amounts to about 50 million tonnes, nearly all of which is obtained from the relatively shallow and accessible waters of the Continental Shelves. It is estimated that this tonnage could probably be expanded by 50 per cent, but that beyond that point overfishing and consequent diminution of production would be serious problems. If the world catch continues to increase at its present rate of 6 per cent per annum, saturation point will be reached within the foreseeable future. Research laboratories in many countries are therefore searching for alternative marine foods, including edible fish such as blue whiting which are at present largely neglected, and exotic sea-foods such as squid, seaweed and plankton. At the same time experiments in 'fish-farming' and in 'farming the sea-bed' are annually increasing in number, and the lessons learnt from these projects suggest that it might ultimately be possible to alter the whole pattern of the world fishing economy. The long-term trend is likely to be away from the present almost exclusive dependence on hunting and collecting and towards more scientific breeding, 'cultivation' and 'cropping'.

SOME FISH NOT YET FULLY EXPLOITED	
Species	Some locations where known to exist in large numbers
Mackerel and Sardines	Persian Gulf, Arabian Sea, Sea of Japan
Hake	Off Patagonia, British Columbia, New Zealand and South Africa
Blue Whiting	Off western Ireland and western Scotland
Perch	Tropical waters, especially in vicinity of coral reefs
Conger Eels and Wrasse	North-west European waters
Flatfish	Off Labrador

Listed above are details of various fish species which are not yet fully exploited. Reasons for this neglect vary, but include the fact that many people do not eat fish and other marine creatures simply because they are not familiar with them as food. For instance squid are readily eaten in

Mediterranean countries and in Japan, but are rarely seen in markets elsewhere, even though they are known to exist in great numbers in most sea areas. Another largely neglected source of marine food is the shrimp. At the present time Russian and Japanese scientists are investigating the food potentialities of the Antarctic krill (*Euphausia superba*)—a small shrimp about 5 cm long which is the main diet of baleen whales. In the cold waters of the Southern Ocean these shrimps are known to exist in vast numbers: in fact it seems likely that at least 50 million tonnes of krill could be caught annually without danger of overfishing. This figure equals the total world marine fish catch, and so it represents a large potential source of food. Krill can be converted into an acceptable animal feed or, after the shells have been removed, be consumed directly as human food in the form of a fish paste. The Japanese already make good use of shrimps, together with other marine creatures, seaweed and vegetables to prepare a traditional dish called *tempura*. To meet the large demand for *tempura* ingredients, successful 'shrimp-farming' experiments have recently been conducted. 'Wheel shrimps' (*Penaeus japonicus*) are trawled from shallow coastal waters and the egg-bearing females—some of which are 23 cm long—are saved for breeding. Each female then produces about 500 000 eggs which are hatched under carefully regulated conditions of temperature, salinity and aeration in specially constructed tanks. The eggs hatch after about 13 hours and the tiny shrimps are fed firstly on diatoms—a variety of plankton—and later on oyster eggs and larvae, brine shrimps, clam eggs and ground vegetable meal. As the shrimps grow they are transferred from the tanks to rearing ponds, from which mature shrimps are eventually harvested by means of a trawl net. The time taken to produce a 'crop' of marketable shrimps is ten months, and the experiments show that large-scale breeding would give a yield of 10 tonnes of shrimps to the hectare.[1] This confirms the opinion of Lionel A. Walford that

> ... a properly constructed artificial brackish water enclosure can be handsomely profitable. ... With the same kind of care that the farm-land requires, that is, careful selection of stock, removal of predators, and fertilizing and

[1] See Alexander McKee, *Farming the Sea*, Souvenir Press, London, p. 146.

feeding, a brackish pond can produce better than three times as much flesh as can an acre of land. That is by using present information. What might result if as much research were put into brackish farming as has already gone into agriculture, no one can say.[2]

Many Oriental countries have a long history of semi-scientific aquaculture in enclosed ponds and coastal lagoons. For instance fish ponds in Hong Kong, where population pressures are especially difficult, produce an annual yield of 3·3 tonnes to the hectare. The photograph opposite shows Malayan peasant farmers inspecting a haul of fresh-water fish taken from their fish-breeding pond. The potentialities for developing shallow brackish-water fish-farming are enormous, for vast areas of tidal lagoons and mangrove swamps at present lie neglected, especially in Indonesia, northern Australia, Oceania and West Africa. One of the most suitable species for this type of cultivation is the milkfish (*Chanos chanos*), a silver relative of the herring which lives in the warm waters of the Indian and Pacific Oceans. A great advantage of the milkfish is that it is completely vegetarian in its feeding habits and so there is no danger of cannibalism in the confined waters of a fish-farm. Milkfish feed on algae which can be collected in great quantities from shallow-water lagoons. The fish are very hardy, and breed in enormous numbers, each female producing from 3 to 5 million eggs at a spawning. The eggs are collected from shallow coastal waters and transferred to enclosed lagoons for hatching. The fry grow very rapidly, reaching a mature marketable weight in sixteen weeks. In Indonesia

> ... ponds are constructed to take advantage of the tide, so that the water is being continually changed. The incoming water carries with it, among other things, very young prawns. These animals characteristically drift into the rich water of the swamps, where they spend their young stages. Thus those that get into the ponds grow there, and when the time comes for their seaward migration they get caught in the traps which the fish farmers have installed for that purpose. The young of various species of fishes also drift into the ponds with the incoming tides. Among these are mullet, which are slow-growing, vegetarians, and also predatory fishes, like *Lates*, which are a nuisance because they feed on milkfishes and prawns.

[2] Chief, Branch of Fishing Biology, U.S. Fish and Wildlife Service.

Crabs get into the ponds, too; they are very good for food, but very damaging to the dykes. By proper construction of the ponds, farmers can keep out predatory and otherwise harmful species; and by proper management they can improve the productivity of their ponds and the profits therefrom.[3]

In Denmark freshwater ponds have been used for commercial fish-farming since the late 19th century. Hitherto production has been geared mainly to the rearing of freshwater trout for the luxury market. The principal fish involved is the American Rainbow trout (*Salmo irideus*), which was brought over from America in 1880 because it grows faster than European varieties, and also because it is hardier and less liable to succumb to fish diseases and parasites. The cultivated trout are given a diet of freshly caught sea-fish. In recent years the business has greatly expanded, due to the fact that modern refrigerated transport has opened up export markets, notably in western Europe and the U.S.A.: 99 per cent of the total Danish cultivated fish catch is exported. Today there are nearly 1000 trout farms in Denmark, mostly located in Jutland where the sticky boulder clay soils favour pond construction. Most of the trout reared are of the freshwater variety, but due to increasing difficulties in finding suitable inland sites Danish fish-farmers are now experimenting with saltwater Rainbow trout in enclosed stretches of brackish sea-water.

... the Ringkøping Fjord is a good example. There is little tidal effect, because the Fjord is cut off from the North Sea by tide gates, and the water is approximately half salt, half fresh. The farms built inside the Fjord consist basically of long, narrow channels excavated in a sandy bottom and are up to 300 yards long by some 15 or 20 yards wide, their sides revetted with wood. Concrete sluices at both ends, with a suction pump at the outlet end, enable water flow to be controlled. Internally, the channels are divided into compartments by screens. The young fish are put into them when they are still small enough to adapt to salt water, the feeding methods being similar to those in use on the freshwater farms. Other farms have been established on the Baltic coast of Denmark where, unlike the North Sea, there are virtually no tidal fluctuations to contend with and the sea is naturally brackish also. Unlike the freshwater farms, the salt-

[3] Fairfield Osborn, *The Limits of the Earth*, Faber & Faber, p. 141.

water experiments are too recent to claim success or to demonstrate failure, although some of the farms have had serious outbreaks of disease among the fish, which is thought to result from the transfer to brackish water. Another disease, known simply as the 'Virus', attacks the fish in the freshwater pond, is highly infectious, and as serious comparatively as foot-and-mouth disease among land cattle.[4]

[4] Alexander McKee, op. cit., p. 104.

A trout farm in Jutland, Denmark. These trout are being separated to obtain their eggs for breeding.

(Above) *Feeding the fish in experimental floating cages at the White Fish Authority, Fish Cultivation Unit, Ardtow, Argyll.*

(Below) *A two-year-old plaice being lifted from a breeding tank.*

Freshwater fish-farms similar to those of Denmark are also found in the U.S.A. and in several west European countries including Switzerland, France, Austria, West Germany and Great Britain. The British White Fish Authority is at present conducting experiments on the rearing of fish in warm salt-water derived from the cooling systems of nuclear power stations located on the coast. This technique represents a new and unconventional trend in a well-established line of fish-farming research in Britain, i.e. the artificial breeding of sea-fish in coastal ponds so that eventually millions of small fry can be released into the sea, there to mature and add to the total fish catch. Such research is being conducted mainly with flatfish, especially plaice at Lowestoft and at Port Erin, Isle of Man.

At first it was very difficult to keep newly hatched fish fry alive in the unnatural environment of a tank or pond, but after painstaking research into the effects of such factors as temperature, salinity, oxygen supply, food and light, the survival rate constantly rose and is now at the astonishingly high proportion of 70 per cent—i.e. it is several hundred times higher than that of fry which hatch in the open sea. According to Dr. O. E. Sette[1] one female mackerel produces 500 000 offspring, of which on average all but twenty perish within two months of spawning. At the end of another eighty-five days *only two* fry from the original half a million eggs are still alive, i.e. the mortality rate amongst mackerel larvae and small-fry is 10–14 per cent per day. The chance that any one egg will grow into a mature edible fish is obviously remote in the extreme.

With this in mind the case for on-shore hatcheries and breeding ponds seems unanswerable, but critics complain (a) that the release of even sizeable fry cannot guarantee that most of them will not promptly be eaten by predators such as larger fish and crabs, and (b) that enormous and impracticable numbers of fry would need to be bred and released to make any appreciable increase in the open sea fish catch—e.g. it would be necessary to liberate at least 1000 million artificially reared young plaice into the North Sea in order to double the catch of plaice made there in any season. One answer to such problems would be to rear sea-fish right up to maturity in on-shore ponds. In fact plaice have been reared up to eatable size in the laboratory at Port Erin, but at a cost in food, labour, power, equipment and overheads far exceeding their market price. Even so, the entire North Sea catch of plaice (about 35 million tonnes p.a.) could be accommodated in shallow ponds extending over 3·2 square kilometres. The potentialities of this type of fish-farming are obvious, but experts at Port Erin reckon that it will be ten years before useful crops of sea-fish can be reared, and even longer for such ventures to be possible on an economic footing in competition with fish caught by conventional methods.

Attempts to establish fish-farms in the open sea are at present in progress in countries as

1 Quoted by, Prof. Gunnar Thorson in 'Fight and Competition on the Sea Bed', see *The Under-sea Challenge*, British Sub-Aqua Club.

widely spread as Japan, the U.S.A. and, on a very minor scale, in Britain. The basic principle underlying all of these schemes is essentially the same, i.e. to create an underwater environment optimal to the breeding of one or more species of marine organism. Experiments so far have mainly concerned creatures which live on the sea-bed, e.g. crayfish, sea-cucumbers, sea-urchins, mussels, oysters and lobsters, but there is much evidence to suggest that similar techniques can also be applied to free-swimming fish. The main method is to establish an underwater 'reef', to provide innumerable artificial nooks and crannies in which sea-creatures can take refuge to eat and multiply. In the open ocean many fish congregate at natural reefs and ledges and in fact a great many species of fish and crustaceans are 'cave-based'. In Japan artificial reefs known as *tsukiiso* and *gyosho*—according to whether they are in shallow or deep water, respectively—are constructed with such materials as concrete pipes, boulders, baulks of timber, oil-drums and old car bodies. In Tokyo Bay, for example,

> . . . one reef consisted of 60 separate concrete 'prefabs' closely grouped and set down near an established crayfish ground at a depth of from 4 to 5 metres. . . . The units were shaped like truncated pyramids with a base 2 metres square and standing 1·5 metres high. They were hollow, but 15 cm diameter pipes were set into their walls, in various patterns, as potential crayfish 'homes'. The crayfish promptly obliged. Although that area had produced very few crayfish previously, the artificial reef not merely increased the numbers present on the barren ground, it actually attracted more lobsters than were to be found on a natural crayfish ground nearby. It also produced a fine crop of commercial seaweed.[2]

Since 1957 the Japanese experiments have been copied in Hawaii, California and the Gulf of Mexico. These American researches have been more successful and have yielded more accurate knowledge because they use trained 'frogmen', i.e. divers equipped with aqua-lungs, masks, flippers and rubber suits to keep out the cold. The divers supervise reef-building and later keep a careful check on the settlement and reproduction rates of the reef's occupants. In Hawaii, for example, in the lee of Oahu Island, three patches

of sea-bed almost devoid of fish life were selected for reef construction, one at 10·5 m, one at 21 m, and the third at 25·5 m. The reefs were built of reinforced concrete slabs, each of which contained cavities in imitation of natural crevices. The shallowest reef was promptly destroyed by surf during a severe storm, but the deeper reefs survived and after a year a fish count was made. The number of fish in the vicinity of the 21 m reef had increased by only 4 per cent—probably due to the fact that it was located on a portion of the sea-bed containing natural hollows and coral 'forests' affording natural hiding places—but the water at the deepest reef showed an astonishing gain in fish of 1910 per cent. A new reef was then built using 549 old car bodies, anchored to the sea-bed with concrete slabs. A fish count on this reef after seven months showed a gain from 40·5 kg to 1734·8 kg per hectare. Long-term

2 Alexander McKee, op. cit., p. 54.

(Top) *A sheephead under the seat of a bus forming part of a man-made fishing reef in 18 m of water off Redondo Beach, California.*

(Bottom) *Kelp bass and a sheephead residing in an automobile reef off Santa Catalina Island, California.*

observations clearly showed that the effect of reef building was to turn a previously barren area into one which was highly productive of edible fish.[1] Additional evidence of the effectiveness of artificial reefs in attracting fish comes from Alabama, where a dry dock sunk in 21 metres of water has become a veritable 'Mecca' for Alabama Gulf Coast Fishing.

Since 1951 the Massachusetts State Hatchery and Research Station at Vineyard Haven has reared millions of lobsters in ponds and then liberated them in the open sea, hoping that this would result in substantial catches by fishermen along the coast. Results so far are inconclusive, partly because no effective means of tagging lobsters has yet been devised (they shed their shells), and partly because it takes six years for a newly liberated lobster to grow to maturity, during which time it can move far away from the place where it was released. In 1966 an experimental fish-farm for lobsters was established by Alexander McKee in an old wooden-hulled wreck, 10 metres down on the sea-bed of Southampton Water. McKee planted old rubber tyres and curved tiles inside the wreck to provide living quarters for the crustaceans. Early catches were encouraging but unfortunately the farm was destroyed by trawling and no accurate assessment of its value can be made. A smaller farm built later showed promise, but it was raided by other fishermen and abandoned. McKee states[2] that in his opinion there is plenty of scope for the establishment of crustacean farms around the coasts of Britain but that before such schemes can become economic potential farmers must be able to obtain (a) leases on those portions of sea-bed on which their farms are to be located, and (b) protection from theft by the establishment of a waterborne police flotilla. Sheltered inlets such as those along the Essex coast and the Helford River in Cornwall, which are used for cultivating oysters, are relatively easy to supervise: with remoter parts of the sea-bed constant surveillance is impossible. Any scheme to cultivate crustaceans or fish in the open sea must also take into account the innumerable predators of eggs, fry and even of large fish which take such an enormous toll of marine life. Crabs, snails, sea-shells, worms, starfish, seals, cor-morants, sharks—the long list of carnivores is in itself an indication of the problem. No effective measures have yet been devised either to keep predators away from a portion of oceanic water or to keep selected species of free-swimming fish within confined limits. Experiments with underwater electronic barriers show promise, but are not yet a commercial proposition.

All of the immense variety of marine creatures which yield human food are derived ultimately from plants, mostly in the form of tiny phytoplankton and—to a much lesser extent—seaweed. The rather larger zooplankton (i.e. animal plankton) feed on the phytoplankton, and above these come fish and crustaceans which eat both zooplankton and weed. Many of the most highly prized edible fish such as the cod prey on smaller fish and so are several stages removed from the primary plant production. At each stage of the food chain there is a heavy loss of food matter, so that whereas estimates suggest that the total production of marine plants is about 130 000 million tonnes, the total annual production of first- and later-stage carnivores is only about 3500 million tonnes, of which only some 350 million tonnes are over the traditional fishing areas of the Continental Shelves. From the point of view of maximizing food output it is therefore clearly economical to catch and use animals which have a fairly short food chain, or even to collect plants such as phytoplankton and seaweed. Plant and animal plankton can be caught in simple trawl devices and zooplankton has long been used as food along the coasts of China and Scandinavia. Phytoplankton, though not a particularly appetizing food, is nevertheless palatable and hunger-satisfying. It has on occasion kept shipwrecked sailors alive, and the crew of the well-known Kon-Tiki expedition used it as a regular food for several months. In fact plankton is a valuable food, containing about 55 per cent protein, 15 per cent fat, 15 per cent carbohydrate, as well as being rich in minerals and vitamins: it is, after all, the only food of the great blue whale, which grows to a length of 21 metres or more in five years. Clearly Man could make immensely greater use of plankton, but there is great difficulty in marketing such an unusual and mostly tasteless food. Probably it will be best to concentrate on using it as an animal feed. At present, however, the thousands of millions of tonnes of plankton are virtually

[1] Iris Unger, *Artificial Reefs*, American Littoral Society, 1966.
[2] In a private communication to the author.

neglected as a direct source of human nutrition, even though it is readily accessible over the Continental Shelves, and also close inshore at the points of upwelling along subtropical 'cold water coasts'.

A possible use for plankton and less attractive fish lies in the preparation of fish protein concentrate (FPC).

As the name suggests this has a very high protein content and, unlike fish meal, is suitable for direct consumption by people. FPC is also dry and keeps indefinitely; it can be prepared in areas where fish are abundant and transported conveniently with very little, if any, wastage to the areas of greatest need. FPC is tasteless and odourless, making it suitable as an additive to other foods which may lack protein constituents essential to an adequate diet. But, of course, FPC costs money and the most promising use for it in the hungry half of the world is in situations such as direct welfare feeding, where the extra cost of protein-enriched food is borne by governments or institutions. FPC may even be added to food such as breakfast cereals in developed countries and, since it cannot impart a taste of fish to eggs or meat, it can also widen the market for fish in animal feeds. Lowering the production costs of attractive foods, and so making them available to people who at present can rarely afford them, might be the most permanent way in which FPC will help to solve the problem of world hunger.[3]

Seaweed, too, could make a significant contribution towards the world's stock of food. It is present in enormous quantities in virtually all coastal waters, is very fast growing and easy to gather, and is rich in carbohydrates, proteins, minerals and trace elements. In the Orient and Oceania certain seaweeds are used as vegetables, but most of them are not digestible by Man. Animals, however, do not have this problem; for example sheep in coastal pastures commonly browse on weeds exposed at low tide, sometimes preferring them to land-grown plants. Seaweed also makes valuable fertilizer, and it is in this capacity that it could probably be used most effectively to help boost world food production.

In the short run, however, it seems certain that the biggest yields of aquatic foods will come from an extension of pond-fish culture. Research conducted since 1957 at the Commonwealth

[3] J. A. Gulland, 'The Ocean Reservoir' Science Journal, May 1968.

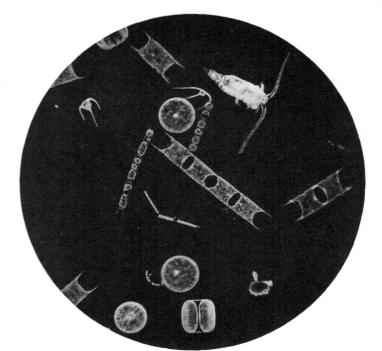

Diatomaceous plankton (magnified about 50 times). These microscopic floating plants are eaten by copepods (minute crustaceans) and are swallowed in myriads by mussels, oysters and other filter-feeding animals. Plankton may also be eaten by man, but despite their valuable protein content they are not very appetizing.

Tropical Fish Culture Research Institute at Batu Berendam, Malacca, proves conclusively that a hectare of pond-water can produce as much food as a hectare of land, and that in Malaya alone more than 200 000 hectares of neglected swamp could be made to yield excellent 'crops' of fish. The Institute, one of the biggest and best equipped of its kind, was deliberately located in Malaya to stand between three distinct types of fish culture—the Chinese carp, Indian carp and Indonesian-Philippines brackish water cultures. The Malaccan site at *pokok gelam* swamp was chosen because it lies near an airport (for easy despatch and receipt of live specimens) and has local supplies of both river and brackish water. Today the Institute contains 164 ponds ranging in size from 100m² to 2ha and the results of its experiments, together with recommendations about new methods of pond culture are published in advisory leaflets. These pioneer methods give promise of 'quite astonishing' increases in tropical fish-farm yields.[4]

[4] Dr. G. A. Prowse, Director, Batu Berendam Institute quoted by Ismail bin Abdullah in 'The Fish Farmers', The Straits Times Annual, 1966, p. 105.

Acknowledgements

We wish to thank the following for permission to reproduce copyright photographs and material (page numbers in brackets):

Aerofilms (frontispiece, 16 (top), 62, 71, 75, 77 (bottom), 83)
A. I. D., Bad Godesberg (106)
Author (p. 3 (top))
Australian News and Information Bureau (17, 40–41, 42)
Barnaby's Picture Library (79, 90 (bottom))
Anne Bolt (31, 32, 35, 87 (bottom), 97 (bottom left))
J. Allan Cash (28, 33, 44, 45, 46 (bottom), 66, 87 (middle), 97 (top))
C.S.I.R.O. (56)
Danish Embassy (115 (bottom))
Danish Tourist Board (67 (bottom))
Prof D. W. Dwyer (65 (top)) from his article in *Geographical Journal*, Vol. CXXVIII, Part 2.
Eyre: *Vegetation and Soils*, Arnold (67 (top))
Forestry Commission (63)
H. W. Gardner, Agriculture Consultant (91)
Geography (107, 108)
Israel Desalination Engineering (Zarchin Process) Ltd, Tel Aviv (54)
Japanese Embassy (95)
Eric Kay (40)
Keystone Press Agency Ltd. (3 (bottom right), 26)
Landestopographie, Bern (108)
Monitor Press Features Ltd. (3 (bottom left), 11, 46 (top), 47)
Paul Popper Ltd. (39, 87 (top), 89, 90 (top), 97 (bottom right))
Radio Times Hulton Picture Library (96)
Rothamsted Experimental Station, Herts. (84)
Royal Netherlands Embassy (70)
Science Journal, London (58)
State of California Department of Fish & Game and Charles H. Turner (117)
Straits Times Press, Singapore (115 (top))
John Topham Limited (80)
U.S. Bureau of Reclamation (53)
U.S. Department of Agriculture (77 (top))
U.S.I.S. (74)
White Fish Authority, Michael Wood (116)
Douglas P. Wilson (119)

Index

122